RETROSPECT
An Anecdotal History of Sullivan County, New York

RETROSPECT
An Anecdotal History of Sullivan County, New York

JOHN CONWAY

PURPLE MOUNTAIN PRESS
Fleischmanns, New York

For my wife Debbie, who was there from the beginning: advising me, supporting me, assisting me, and in some cases, leading me.

Retrospect: An Anecdotal History of Sullivan County, New York

FIRST EDITION
1996

Published by
PURPLE MOUNTAIN PRESS, LTD.
Main Street, P.O. Box E3
Fleischmanns, New York 12430-0378
914-254-4062
914-254-4476 (fax)

Copyright © 1996 by John Conway

All rights reserved under International and Pan-American Copyright Conventions. No part of this book may be reproduced or transmitted in any form without permission in writing from the publisher and copyright holder.

Library of Congress Cataloging-in-Publication Data

Conway, John, 1952--
    Retrospect : an anecdotal history of Sullivan County, New York / John Conway. -- 1st ed.
    p.   cm.
    ISBN 0-935796-72-X (pb : acid-free paper)
    1. Sullivan County (N.Y.)--History--Anecdotes.   I. Title.
F127.S91C66   1996
974.7'35--dc20   96-14374
                                                                             CIP

Manufactured in the United States of America on acid-free paper.
1 3 5 7 9 8 6 4 2

Cover: Night Illumination, Entrance---Amusement Park, Monticello, N.Y.
(Post card courtesy Sullivan County Historical Society)
Back cover: Photograph of the author by Chris Ramirez/The Record.

TABLE OF CONTENTS

Acknowledgments 7
Introduction 9

Chapter One: Some Personalities and Events
    That Have Shaped Our County

Street Wise 11
The War Hits Home 12
Judge Thornton Offers a Bribe 14
'Valley of the Spring' 16
A Railroad Magnate's Princely Preserve 18
Who Was Ruddick Trowbridge? 20
The Patriotic Train 21
Henry Morrison Flagler 23
The Passing of Abe Deutsch 24
George L. Cooke 26
Judith Smith Kaye 28

Chapter Two: Places of Interest

Readers are Last Resort in Search for First 30
Crude Oil 33
Excelsior 35
Residents Resisted Tuberculosis Retreats 38
Monticello Industries in the Early 1900s 40
Fancy Glass 44
The Saga of the Delaware Ferry 46
Passenger Pigeons 53
Memories of Majestic Mongaup Falls 54
Cowboys, Alligators and Renegade Bison 56
The Liberty Highway 58
Sullivan Was Slow to Enter the Fast Lane 60
A Cop on a Harley 62

Chapter Three: Recreation

The Art of Chewing's Blackest Era	65
Fishing With Your Bare Hands?	68
Home of Spalding Bats	71
The Hemlocks	77
Memories of Monticello Amusement Park	81

Chapter Four: Slices of Life

Barbershops: Shear Pleasure	85
Pioneer Physicians: The Stuff of Legends	88
Shoemakers?	91
One-Woman Schools	93
Carriage Makers	94
Drug Stores Were Fewer, Farther Between	96
Resort Advertising Reflects Times	98
Old Remedies, Lawyers and Cheap Coffins	104
Year of the Great Sesquicentennial	110

Chapter Five: Entertainment

Mongaup, Movies and Murder	113
Caesar Gets Votes for Comedy Hall of Fame	115
Berlin's Local Legacy	119
Scandal	121
Sonny Liston	126
Boxing and the Catskills	127

Chapter Six: Crime and Punishment

Edward C. Dollard: Hero Cop	133
Gangland Killing Led to Courtroom Dramatics	135
Drucker Trial Opened Syndicate Can of Worms	138
Mobster May Have Thrown Away Millions	145
Mob Legend Waxey Pops Up at Rocky's	147

Acknowledgments

RETROSPECT was born in the summer of 1987, and was originally envisioned as a short-lived series of reminiscences of a young man who had come of age in the era of the big hotels in Sullivan County. With the help of a legion of people, it has evolved into something quite different, and is, nearly nine years later, still going strong.

Some of those who have made the column—and therefore this book—possible deserve mention here: My wife Debbie, who not only helped me reach the right editors in my attempt to pitch the column idea in the first place, but provided invaluable assistance throughout; Alan Barrish, the director of the Crawford Public Library in Monticello, who has always looked for the books I've needed, no matter how obscure; Bert Feldman, who whetted my appetite for local history initially; the late Paul Gerry, who never turned down a project; Gary Grossman, former executive editor at the Middletown *Times Herald-Record*, for granting permission to reprint the columns; Amanda Luke and Laura Dolce, my editors at the *Times Herald-Record;* Rich Newman, Rick Newman, Yits Kantrowitz, Ben Kaplan, Del Van Etten, Mary Curtis, Austin Smith, William and Barbara O'Rourke, and Wray and Loni Rominger and their staff at Purple Mountain Press. Others, too numerous to mention, have been only slightly less invaluable by providing ideas and memories, photos and old newspapers, support and inspiration. As I've always said, these are my partners in this endeavor. Many thanks to all.

Introduction

THERE must be a strong trace of dignity in recording history. It should arise from a constant penchant for truth and a desire to rekindle and enjoy the thoughts of others from other times. Every safeguard must be taken, lest it be adulterated by baseness or cheapened by inaccuracy. In the allotment of credit or discredit to the men and women who have walked into the spotlight on its stage, there is a sacred responsibility.

This history of Sullivan County, a recital of events and people affecting it over a given period, is colorful and reflective of those who have lived and labored within it. It is a treasury of impressive accounts, glistening with characteristic Americana.

By assaying these accounts, we are able to appreciate the talents and the sacrifices of those who preceded us. More importantly, we are able to see our own road ahead and to avoid the mistakes and capitalize on the triumphs of those who went before. We are not interested so much in the doings and deaths of the monarchies, but more in the inward spirit that has motivated normal people in the normal labyrinthine ways of earthy life.

We have been fortunate. Our historical appetites have been whetted and gratified by Quinlan's *History of Sullivan County*, published in 1873 and heralded by several as one of the best local histories. It is recognizable by its flowery Victorian expression, its thoroughness and its exactitude. Mention is also required of Child's *Gazetteer and Business Directory of Sullivan County*, printed a year earlier. Its wealth of facts and charts are compactly arranged by towns. A panoramic picture of the region in different days can be drawn from the large number of revealing advertisements and demographic listings. To be sure, others have written well, but their scope of the past has been more limited in period or subject.

RETROSPECT

Now comes John Conway with *An Anecdotal History of Sullivan County*. Born and raised in the area about which he writes with consuming affection, the author has a rich background in its print and sound media in general--and in history, in its particular. The volume is a magnificent contribution to the authentic lore of bygone days. It seems to pick up where Quinlan terminated.

The keen mind and facile pen of the author are revealed in the widespread variety and logical arrangement of the narratives which pass in review. Classified in groups such as recreation, personalities, events, places, interesting businesses and callings, an informal and delightful mental picture of Sullivan County is offered readers. Actual photographs of county scenes and personalities support the text.

John Conway has accomplished his mission. He has devoted a large slice of his life to scholarly research and recording. His very commendable work should be digested with relish for the past and a resolve to improve upon the attainments of those from whom we have taken up the torch.

Lawrence H. Cooke, Chief Judge
New York State Court of Appeals (Retired)

Chapter One

Some Personalities and Events that Have Shaped Our County

Street Wise

OF ALL THE WRITERS to come out of Sullivan County, few are of greater stature that Alfred B. Street of Monticello. Many ranked him behind only Bryant, Longfellow, Halleck and Emerson among American poets of his time.

Although Street was born in Poughkeepsie in 1811 and lived the latter part of his life in Albany, he grew up in Monticello, and he gained his inspiration from the area around that picturesque village. In fact, some of his most well-known pieces are descriptive narratives of people, places and events from the Monticello of the early 1800s. One of Street's most respected poems is "Walk and Pic-Nic," in which he takes the reader on a stroll from Monticello to Pleasant Pond (now Kiamesha Lake).

"Walk and Pic-Nic" and other narratives made such an impact on critics of the time that they placed Street at the forefront of American descriptive poets. *The Foreign Quarterly Review*, a British literary publication, placed Street "at the head of his class." The journal proclaimed, "His pictures of American Scenery are full of gusto and freshness; sometimes too wild and diffuse, but always true and healthful." Similar praise came from other literary publications as well. James Eldridge Quinlan, noted author and historian, called Street's poetry "but a reflex of his daily walk in Sullivan."

Street came to Monticello with his family in 1825, when he was fourteen, the same year his first publications, his poems "March" and "A Winter Noon," appeared in the New York *Evening Post*. He lived in Monticello until 1839, when he left for Albany and a position as state librarian. He served in that capacity for nearly thirty years.

The beauty and tranquillity of the woods and streams surrounding Monticello remained etched in his memory, and he made cherished, if infrequent, visits to his erstwhile home. It is difficult, if not impossible, to separate Street's renown as a poet from his life as a resident of Monticello, the two are so closely intertwined. Quinlan, recalling an article about Street published in *Graham's Magazine*, related the following excerpt concerning the influence of his Monticello home: "The beautiful village of Monticello. . .is situated in a picturesque region of wild hills, smiling valleys, and lovely streams. . . . Early association with such a life gave the first scope and impulse to our poet's mind."

Yet, as is the case with many other local notables, Street is all but ignored in the educational process; surely, most current residents are unaware of his achievements. Shouldn't the accomplishments of those such as Street—and Frederick Cook and Stephen Crane, men from Sullivan County who made their marks in American history—be taught in our local school system? Aren't their indisputable contributions to history and literature worthy of note? Of course they are. Figures such as these should be the foundation upon which a course in local history is built and made available to students in all districts. After all, history is still history even if it has the misfortune to occur in our own backyard.

Just as Alfred B. Street was enriched by his association with Monticello, and built a notable reputation for his ability to relate his appreciation of the beauty of Sullivan County, so might one of today's youth be enriched by hearing of the exploits of such men.

The War Hits Home

A SUDDEN, deafening roar shattered the stillness of the summer afternoon, and then there was silence—absolute, eerie, silence. It was July 15, 1864. Far from Sullivan County, the Civil War raged on, claiming lives and devastating homes and property from Bull Run to Gettysburg. But like most northern locales, this area remained relatively untouched by the conflict.

PERSONALITIES AND EVENTS

If anything, the war was actually *helping* the county: The tanning industry was thriving because of the army's need for leather. And although Sullivan County had answered President Lincoln's call for troops, forming the 143rd Regiment, the tanning industry remained the area's primary link—indirect as it was—to the war. That is, until that July Friday afternoon.

At 2:45 p.m., on a blind curve on the Erie line near Shohola, just across the Delaware River from Barryville, a train carrying 125 Union troops and 800 Confederate prisoners of war on their way to a prison camp at Elmira collided head-on with a loaded coal train.

The coal train had been placed on the Erie tracks in Hawley. It should have been stopped at Lackawaxen, since the dispatcher there had known the prison train was approaching from the east. But the dispatcher at Lackawaxen was drunk that afternoon, and the coal train was allowed to continue eastward without any warning.

The force of the collision raised both engines into the air; when they settled back to earth, the locomotive of the coal train was crushed beneath the pile. The engineer of the coal train had jumped clear just prior to the impact. The engineer and the fireman of the prisoners' train were not so fortunate; they were both killed in the collision.

There was even more devastation farther back along the line of cars. The first box car on the train had housed thirty-eight prisoners. It was so badly crushed in the wreck that only one of them survived. Most of the other eighteen occupied cars were less severely damaged, but casualties were nonetheless heavy.

Local residents, many of whom were alerted by the terrible sound of the collision, soon arrived on the scene. From Shohola and Barryville, townspeople turned out to pull the injured from the train and tend to them. Upon the arrival of a rescue train with railroad employees and medical personnel, the dead were buried in trenches dug along the tracks. The volunteers helped transport 123 injured prisoners and guards, as well as those who were not hurt in the wreck, to the Shohola railroad station and the Shohola Glen Hotel.

Several Confederate soldiers managed to escape. Prisoners who were thought well enough to travel were sent on another train to Elmira; those too seriously injured to be moved stayed in Shohola, where two of them later died.

Those two Confederate soldiers—brothers—are buried in the cemetery at the Congregational Church in Barryville. "That's how it came that there are two Confederate soldiers killed during the Civil War buried here in Sullivan County," says Town of Highland historian Austin Smith. "And these two boys, the Johnson brothers, have all but been forgotten."

But not by Smith, whose own grandfather fought in the War Between the States. Smith doesn't make a big deal of it, but each Memorial Day he makes the trek up the hill to the tiny cemetery and quietly places a small Confederate flag on each of the graves. "They're soldiers, just like anyone else," Smith says, "And they don't deserve to be totally forgotten."

The prisoners and guards buried in the trenches along the railroad tracks stayed there until 1911, when the remains were moved to Elmira. "The federal government sponsored the disinterment," Smith says. "They found some of the graves had been washed out by floods over the years, but those remains they could find they moved to Woodlawn National Cemetery. The graves there—seventeen Union soldiers and forty-nine Confederates—are marked by what's called the Shohola Monument."

And though there is no monument in Barryville, Austin Smith faithfully sees that the two graves there are marked each year, as well.

Judge Thornton Offers a Bribe

RETIRED CHIEF JUDGE of the New York State Court of Appeals Lawrence H. Cooke is, among other things, a walking encyclopedia of Sullivan County history. Judge Cooke has favored me with a number of fascinating stories over the years, one of which became particularly appropriate when Pierre Rinfret ran for New York state governor.

"I think you'll find it interesting," Judge Cooke promised, directing me to a newspaper story with a headline, "Rinfret Says He'll Take $1 a Year Salary as Governor."

"It kind of brings back memories of Judge Thornton, doesn't it?" the judge asked, referring to a story he had told me a few days before as we walked through the Sullivan County Courthouse. And he was

PERSONALITIES AND EVENTS

right. It was impossible to read the story about Rinfret's promise without recalling the saga of Judge Thornton.

William L. Thornton was running for Sullivan County Court Judge in 1878 when he made a rather unusual campaign promise: "If elected to the office of county judge, I will pledge myself to take only $1,200 a year for my services," Thornton said, forsaking the $2,500 annual salary allotted for the position. "I will pay out of my own pocket the coal necessary to heat my law office, I will pay for all stationery and letterheads, and I will see that people needing blanks pay for them themselves."

The electorate apparently liked Thornton's idea of fiscal restraint, and he won the office by a 3,211 to 2,947 vote over incumbent Timothy F. Bush. But the fun was just beginning: Bush protested the election, claiming that Thornton had, in effect, bribed the electorate with his promise to accept less than the designated salary for the office.

The case came before Judge Osborne in state Supreme Court in May 1880. Bush pleaded his own case along with Benjamin Reynolds, while James L. Stewart and C. V. R. Ludington represented Thornton. Judge Osborne ruled in Bush's favor, and invalidated the election, holding that Thornton's promise violated Article 12 of the New York State Constitution. Osborne wrote:

> If one, in order to obtain his election, may offer to give to the taxpayers directly or indirectly one-half of his legal salary as an inducement for the giving or withholding of votes, he can certainly offer to give the whole of such salary. Nor would it end here. If this can be done; if the courts will tolerate such practices, then there is nothing to prevent an aspirant for any elective office within the gift of the people...not only to discharge its duties gratuitously, but in addition thereto to promise any amount he may be willing to pay...and from no other or higher motive than thus to influence and corrupt their votes.

Judge Osborne, it might be noted, also took the opportunity to pat himself on the back with an unusual postscript to his decision: "The questions discussed in this opinion are interesting and important, and, so far as I can ascertain, never before the courts of this state for adjudication," he wrote. "I have presented them...to some of the ablest lawyers and jurists in the state, who have without exception concurred in the conclusions I have reached."

Thornton appealed the case, and attorney Thornton A. Niven argued his appeal. The principle of law set forth earlier by Judge Osborne was upheld, although the higher court reversed his decision overturning the election. The Appeals Court ruled that it was incumbent upon Bush to have produced evidence in the trial that there were voters, equal in number to the majority Thornton had received, who voted for Thornton expressly because of the improper influence of his promise. Bush had produced no such witnesses.

Thornton remained in office and served admirably as county court judge. His name, meanwhile, is forever linked in legal annals to just what "bribing the electorate" entails.

'Valley of the Spring'

IT'S IMPOSSIBLE for me to drive through Glen Spey without thinking of George R. McKenzie. McKenzie was the multi-millionaire Singer Sewing Machine Company executive who not only provided Glen Spey with its name, but constructed a number of the hamlet's most beautiful buildings.

When McKenzie came to Sullivan County around 1870, he was the vice president and general manager of the Singer Manufacturing Company, founded by Isaac Merrit Singer, and, following the settlement of a lawsuit filed by Elias Howe, America's leading producer of sewing machines. McKenzie settled in a secluded, almost desolate part of the county then known as South Lebanon, and almost immediately renamed it Glen Spey—"valley of the spring" roughly translated from Scottish.

McKenzie eventually owned more than 3,000 acres of woodland, including a parcel at the corner of County Road 42 and Proctor Road, where he decided to build his home. But it wasn't just *any* home. McKenzie was one of the wealthiest men ever to reside in Sullivan County, and he spared no expense. He erected a magnificent, enormous mansion, and surrounded it with exquisite landscaping.

The Homestead, as the estate became known, was truly a palace fit for a king. The land around the mansion was terraced, and the shrubbery was meticulously cut into the shapes of various animals. A state-of-the-art golf course was laid out on the grounds, and a pond was created, with an island upon which a small house was constructed for McKenzie's swans. The pond, island, and swan house (or a reasonable facsimile) still exist, and are plainly visible from County Road 42.

No estate would have been complete in those days without a riding stable and carriage house, and McKenzie's Homestead was no exception. True to form, he erected elaborate buildings to serve these functions—so elaborate, in fact, that the structures which once served as McKenzie's stable and carriage house now make up a plush and popular restaurant.

But McKenzie didn't stop there. His own estate finished, he turned his attention to the construction of a church, a school, and a post office. The school building he funded is currently the Lumberland Town Hall.

McKenzie had a large family, and each of his children eventually had an estate of his or her own. Belle McKenzie Craig lived at Thornlebank, currently part of the Bel Air Minsk resort. Margaret McKenzie Elkin was given Bonnie Brae, Grace McKenzie Ewing had Bramble Brae, and Rebecca McKenzie VanDerbeck received Ardmore.

McKenzie's sons—James, Alexander, and Edward—each had an estate as well. Windy Knoll and Wold Croft, which belonged to James and Alexander, respectively, are both still intact and are currently part of the Knights of Pythias camp. They are mammoth buildings, and despite years of use as multiple residences they each still exude a warmth and a charm that make it apparent that a single family would have felt very comfortable living in either of them. Edward McKenzie's home, Bel Air—perhaps the largest of the children's estates—burned to the ground in the 1950s.

A trip through Glen Spey used to last but a moment; now it invariably takes me an afternoon. I pause at the remains of the charred mansions, at the pond with the swan house, and at the Knights of Pythias camp—always catching sight of some detail that escaped me before.

RETROSPECT

A Railroad Magnate's Princely Preserve

OF ALL THE PROMINENT MEN who have figured in the history of Sullivan County, few were as colorful as Chester W. Chapin, Jr., a multi-millionaire railroad and shipping magnate from Connecticut who, around the turn of the century, owned more than 18,000 acres of land in the towns of Highland, Lumberland, Forestburgh and Bethel.

Chapin, who had inherited great wealth from his father and built upon it, was the president of the New Haven Steamboat Company, the Central New England Railway, and several other ventures when he began accumulating land in Sullivan County in 1891. His estate, which he used primarily as a hunting preserve but which he always considered home, included Lebanon and Cliff Lakes, along with several buildings, most notably the stately main house, which is still standing.

He bought most of the acreage cheap—old tax rolls from the town of Highland placed the value of some sections at as little as fifty cents an acre—and much of it had already been built upon. Chapin salvaged whatever buildings he thought worth saving, moving them all together into a group, and had others torn down. He had the main lodge built to his own specifications; it was rustic, but included large quantities of bluestone from local quarries—and indoor plumbing, a rarity in those days.

While the lodge may have paled in comparison with the nearby estates of other millionaires (the Mc-

Chester W. Chapin, Jr. Chapin (far right) is pictured with his wife Emilia in an ox-drawn sled in what is believed to be one of the few surviving photographs of the railroad and steamship magnate who once owned a several-thousand-acre hunting preserve in Sullivan County. (Author's collection)

PERSONALITIES AND EVENTS

Kenzies, the Bradfords, and the Proctors among them), it was, in its own way, just as magnificent. And it still is. "The woodwork in this place is incredible," one man told me. He had inspected the structure while preparing a bid on some electrical work the current owner, Orange and Rockland Utilities, was having done there. "They were planning on duplicating some of the designs; the scroll work, in portions of the wood, must have cost them a fortune." Other contractors I have spoken to who have seen the building support that contention.

The mix of game animals Chapin provided his millionaire hunting cohorts is perhaps as fascinating as anything. He had hundreds of North American elk brought in from Colorado, Kansas and Wyoming, and maintained a healthy herd of white-tailed deer. The elk were brought up on the railroad to Pond Eddy and then herded by hired wranglers, cattle-drive style, to the estate. Chapin segregated the two groups of animals— the elk he kept within a fenced-in area around Lebanon Lake, while the deer were confined to the vicinity of Cliff Lake—and visitors could hunt one or the other. In addition to this big game, Chapin kept his preserve well-stocked with pheasant and fish, especially trout—presumably necessary to entertain such notable friends as C. C. Tiffany, Bradford Lee Gilbert (the architect), and Thomas Edison, all of whom were regular guests at the estate.

Chapin died in 1922, and left a fortune estimated between $2.5 and $5 million; his Sullivan County property was worth about $325,000 at that time. The Public Service Company, which would eventually become Orange and Rockland, purchased 7,000 acres of the property less than a year after Chapin's death, about a year after it had bought Mongaup Falls. Part of the acreage was devoted to the construction of the Swinging Bridge and Mongaup Falls reservoirs, and O&R added considerable new construction, including a private landing strip. But much of the estate, including the lodge, is still very much as Chapin left it.

It stands, enduring and foreboding, at the end of Chapin Road, a couple of miles off County Road 43. But don't plan on getting to see this wonderful remnant of Sullivan County's past—what's left of Chapin's princely preserve is entirely private property, and the utility doesn't welcome sightseers.

RETROSPECT

Who Was Ruddick Trowbridge?

WHO WAS RUDDICK TROWBRIDGE? I'd always ask anyone within earshot whenever I passed the sign marking the Monticello American Legion Hall. I don't think I ever received a satisfying answer until I came across the January 10, 1919, issue of the *Republican Watchman* newspaper.

"Trowbridge Killed at Fismes," the paper's headline read. "Letter From His Lieutenant Tells Monticello Relatives," reads a subhead. Trowbridge's death was considered monumental enough by the editor of the paper that it upstaged an article reporting the death of former president Theodore Roosevelt, who had passed away in his sleep at his home in Oyster Bay, N.Y.

It seems that Ruddick Trowbridge had been reported missing in France in August 1918, and despite exhaustive efforts, nothing more could be learned regarding him. Friends and relatives presumed he had been captured by the Germans and imprisoned. His parents attempted to ascertain his whereabouts, but to no avail. Finally, they wrote to the officer in charge of their son's company.

In his reply, Lieutenant Horace B. Smith wrote: "I am truly grieved to have to notify you that your son was killed in action near Fismes, France on August 10, 1918. My dear Mr. Trowbridge, your son met his death as only heroes can. He was killed instantly by an artillery shell. His bravery, till he met his death, with that of his comrades, has made history. It was the turning of the tide. I truly sympathize with you in your great loss."

So, who was Ruddick Trowbridge? He was born in February, 1895 in the Powell House on West Broadway in Monticello. He attended Monticello High School, where he played baseball and basketball with considerable success. After high school, he participated in both sports in village competition. He moved to California in 1916, but didn't stay long, choosing instead to return to Monticello and work in his father's lumber yard. He enlisted on December 7, 1917, and left Monticello with twelve other volunteers.

Trowbridge ended up in the Machine Gun Company, 30th Infantry, 3rd Division, and was shipped overseas in April 1918. He entered battle in France in June 1918; in July he took part in the great Battle of the Marne, in which the Americans inflicted heavy losses on the Germans, driving them back in a confrontation many considered the turning point of the war. In a letter to his parents dated July 28, Trowbridge recounted his part in the battle: "The following day after the attack, we drove them across the river and now have them on the run. Our whole 3rd Division is to be retired soon and moved back to get filled up with new men. We have been on the front for over a month, living in dugouts. I will be glad to get back to camp and get a bath and some new clothes, as I haven't had my clothes off for over a month." The letter was the last his family would hear from him.

Trowbridge became the second Monticello man killed in action in France. George Wayman was the first, though the *Watchman* noted that Wayman's family was still, at that time, awaiting official confirmation of their son's death.

So who was Ruddick Trowbridge? He was, in the truest sense, an All-American boy, the kind of popular, charismatic youth the grim trench warfare of World War I claimed by the thousands. The *Watchman* rightfully hailed Trowbridge a hero, expressing the popular sentiment of the day in doing so: "He gave his life in a heroic manner, fighting for humanity, and to save the world from Prussianism, and there could be no greater or more worthy cause for any man to lay down his life."

The Patriotic Train

WHAT THE SULLIVAN COUNTY *REPUBLICAN* NEWSPAPER referred to as "probably the biggest day Callicoon has ever seen" occurred in that hamlet on October 2, 1918. That Wednesday marked the arrival in Sullivan County of the federal government's Patriotic Train.

To fully appreciate the magnitude of this event, one must first consider that the country was in the midst of World War I at the time, and although the tide had clearly turned, there was no indication that an end was in sight. The Allies had inflicted significant defeats on the Germans in France throughout September, and in an effort to keep the momentum going President Woodrow Wilson had kicked off the fourth Liberty Loan campaign on September 27 with

RETROSPECT

the words, "War must achieve a peace based on equal justice for all people."

The Patriotic Train was part of that Liberty Loan program. It traveled the country, stopping at big cities and small towns, displaying war souvenirs and the latest weapons. Prominent officials usually accompanied the train and made speeches on behalf of the loan campaign. The train would arrive in a town according to a pre-arranged schedule, and would take part in a day-long celebration in support of the war. Its arrival was usually marked by a parade and other festivities. The train would spend a day at one locality and then move along to its next scheduled stop.

The train was greeted upon its arrival in Callicoon—the train's only layover in Sullivan County—by throngs of people from miles around. The *Republican* reported on the festivities the following Friday: "People from all over the county and many from outside the county including Pennsylvania assembled at Callicoon to see the exhibition, which was well worth going miles to see. It consisted of trophies taken from the Germans as well as samples of much of our fighting equipment which is used abroad and was very instructive as well as interesting."

A massive parade accompanied the whistle stop. The Callicoon Home Defense Corps had organized the march and had recruited other Home Defense Corps to take part. Firemen, rifle clubs, and other civic groups also marched. James H. Curtis, the supervisor of the town of Delaware, delivered the welcome address and led the parade. Curtis was also captain of the Callicoon Home Defense Corps.

Following the parade and train exhibitions, the hamlet held a fund-raising dance at the Western Hotel. "A grand ball was held in the evening at which a great crowd assembled and taken altogether it was a great and gala day for Callicoon," the newspaper proclaimed.

The stop in Callicoon was considered a successful one—over $40,000 worth of Liberty Bonds were sold. These bonds were hawked from the platform of the train, and it was considered a citizen's duty to purchase as many as he could afford. Although the war ended just over a month later, the Liberty Loan campaign was a timely and necessary program to pay off war debts. (The war had been costly—not just in terms of human lives, but in dollars as well. One economist

PERSONALITIES AND EVENTS

at the time estimated World War I cost over $232 *trillion* to fight—about $164 million a day.)

The *Republican* praised the Callicoon celebration as "giving a great impetus to the fourth Liberty Loan drive throughout the county," and it was generally agreed that it would be many years before Callicoon would again host such a large and festive event. In fact, while town meetings were held throughout the county in support of the Liberty Loan campaign, nowhere did a celebration take place that could rival the Callicoon event.

Henry Morrison Flagler

HENRY MORRISON FLAGLER was one of the most successful businessmen in America just prior to the turn of the century. Along with John D. Rockefeller, he founded the Standard Oil Company in 1870, and served as its secretary treasurer. He built a railroad the length of the state of Florida, and constructed a number of luxury hotels.

But the Flagler Hotel in Sullivan County was not among them.

My wife and I had actually done considerable research into Henry Morrison Flagler's life several years ago, while in St. Augustine, Florida, the site of three of his most famous hotels: the Ponce de Leon, the Alcazar, and the Cordova. We were curious if there was some connection between the magnanimous millionaire and Sullivan County's premier hotel of another era. We found nothing to indicate Flagler had ever been to the mountains.

The Flagler Hotel was built in 1872. Carrie Flagler Angel, the daughter of Nicholas Flagler, partner in the Old Falls tannery of Palen and Flagler, was the first proprietor. (Henry Morrison Flagler also had a daughter Carrie, but she died as an infant, sometime around 1865.) And

Henry Morrison Flagler. Although he did not build the Flagler Hotel in South Fallsburg, Henry Morrison Flagler did have a direct link to the area. He was the treasurer of John D. Rockefeller's Standard Oil Company, which constructed a pipeline through the county in the 1870s. (Photo courtesy Memorial Presbyterian Church, St. Augustine, Florida)

23

just in case you're thinking that perhaps Nicholas and Henry were related in some way, we thought of that, too. "We don't have a lot of information about Henry Flagler's early life, because he wasn't from here," Sherry Nivida, the librarian at the St. Augustine Historical Society told me. "But we do have a family tree that someone prepared many years ago and donated to us. There is no Nicholas Flagler anywhere, and no Carrie—other than the one who died as a little girl."

Carrie Flagler Angel operated the thirty-five-room Flagler House, as it was known then, until 1908, when it was purchased by Asias Fleisher and Philip Morgenstern and became a kosher resort that accommodated more than 250 by 1920. It was under Fleisher and Morgenstern that hot and cold running water was introduced and that telephones were installed in every room—features which set the Flagler apart from other area hotels of that era. And, of course, it was under their ownership that the 1,500-seat theater for which the resort was famous was constructed a few years later. Jack Barsky purchased the hotel in 1953.

It makes a good story that millionaire Henry Morrison Flagler had an intimate enough connection to Sullivan County to build one of his hotels here. But it just didn't happen that way.

The Passing of Abe Deutsch

WE KNOW from our history that the first Jewish settlers came to Sullivan County to farm. Finding the soil here rocky and infertile, they soon turned their farm houses into boarding houses—and the Borscht Belt was born.

The story of these Jewish settlers is in many ways the story of Sullivan County. Jewish farmers-turned-innkeepers worked hard—often sixteen to twenty hours a day—and many continued to work their farms to provide foodstuffs for their guests. In later years, some of the boarding houses turned into major hotels, in the process swallowing up the farms that spawned them. Other boarding houses retained their original charm, playing host to succeeding generations of the same families as the years went by.

PERSONALITIES AND EVENTS

Then, slowly at first and later with increasing frequency, the boarding houses began to fade from the scene. The innkeepers passed away—and there was no one to take their place, no one willing to work twenty-hour days, no one who wanted to farm and keep house for the guests when there were much easier ways to make a living. The face of Sullivan County changed with each closing, with each fire, with each death. It changed again when Abe Deutsch passed away.

Unless you lived in Hurleyville, you probably never heard of Abe Deutsch. His was not a large farm. His was not a major hotel. But Abe Deutsch's story is the story of Sullivan County just the same.

His parents, Samuel and Bella, came to Hurleyville to farm, but before long began operating a boarding house—they called it the Applebee Inn—on what was later to become known as Columbia Hill in Hurleyville. The Deutsches were workers, and the Applebee Inn grew steadily. The original building doubled in size, and then outlying buildings were added. And then a swimming pool. And still they farmed.

Sam and Bella had a large family, but it was Abe who stayed on, farming and housekeeping, working the long days, who rose early to gather and deliver eggs to the other Jewish families in the area, who was the last to retire at night after making sure his guests were all tucked in. It was Abe who made the Applebee Inn—and the guests and the farm—his life, and kept at it long after he should have, long after most of the others of his era had faded away.

Now Abe Deutsch is gone, too, and the buildings that were once the Applebee Inn—and later known as Fairlawn Acres—stand vacant, a silent tribute to the life of a man. Those of us who knew Abe Deutsch will not easily forget him. He was quiet and unassuming, and could put you immediately at ease. And, in the true tradition of early Sullivan County, he was always ready to help his neighbors in any way he could. Watch your house while you're away? Absolutely. Mind your animals for a week? Certainly. Help with the haying? Just say the word. Abe Deutsch knew no other way. He became, as Rabbi Irving Goodman pointed out at his funeral, the unofficial mayor of Hurleyville. He had an endless supply of stories from the old days, and, with a twinkle in his eye, he would tell them without much encouragement.

RETROSPECT

When I wanted to know about the gangster Jack Drucker and his ties to the mob, Abe filled me in. When I needed to know where an old hotel had been located, Abe pointed it out. He was a wealth of information, and his son, Stan, always wanted me to record his musings. I never did. Abe Deutsch, farmer, innkeeper, good neighbor, and storyteller, is gone. The face of Sullivan County has changed again, and we've allowed another page of our history to be turned without taking the time to fully absorb or appreciate it.

George L. Cooke

HE WAS BORN AND RAISED IN MONTICELLO, and chose to spend his professional life there, forsaking numerous opportunities to move on. He flawlessly presided over the two most famous trials in Sullivan County history. His name became synonymous with honesty and integrity. And he always had time to chat with a six-year-old boy.

He was Judge George L. Cooke, and a wiser, more decent man never donned the robes of justice.

George L. Cooke was born in Monticello November 9, 1878, the son of Henry A. and Mary Toohey Cooke. He was in the first graduating class at Monticello High School in 1895, and immediately began teaching school, first at Maplewood, and then at Kiamesha Lake. But a law career beckoned irresistibly, and he soon became a clerk to the county court judge and surrogate. He graduated Albany Law School in 1902, and entered private practice a year later.

George L. Cooke. Lawyer, District Attorney, County Court Judge, George L. Cooke epitomized justice. (Photo courtesy Lawrence H. Cooke.)

PERSONALITIES AND EVENTS

While in private practice, George L. Cooke was a people's lawyer, never turning down a client in need. His reputation for compassion and fairness grew quickly, and after stints as justice of the peace and clerk of the board of supervisors, he was elected district attorney in 1909. He did such an admirable and effective job in the office that when it came time to run for reelection in 1912 he did so with the Republican and Bull Moose Party endorsements, as well as that of the Democratic Party.

He had married Mary Elizabeth Pond, a school teacher, in 1910, and eventually fathered two sons: George B. Cooke, who became a respected New York City attorney, and Lawrence H. Cooke, chief judge of the New York State Court of Appeals from 1979 to 1984.

In 1926, George L. Cooke was elected county court judge, a post he held for the next twenty-two years, until he reached the mandatory retirement age of seventy in 1948. It was during his time on the county bench that Judge Cooke achieved widespread fame for his part in breaking up Murder, Incorporated. In 1940, he presided over the trial of Irving "Big Gangi" Cohen, accused in the ice-pick murder of slot machine czar Walter Sage. Cohen's trial, and the 1944 trial of Jack Drucker, who was also charged in the Sage murder, were, by all accounts, judicial masterpieces.

"My father was a seasoned magistrate, and wasn't fazed by the Murder, Incorporated, trials," Judge Lawrence Cooke recalled. "One of the defense attorneys told me years later that my father had presided over the court in wonderful fashion, that the court transcripts revealed a perfect record, leaving the defense attorney no chance for reversal."

Despite his retirement from the bench, Judge George L. Cooke remained active in his community and in the Monticello Fire Department, to which he belonged for more than sixty years. As impressive as his public record was, however, something else will always set him apart in the mind of one who knew him only briefly, through the eyes of a child.

Judge Cooke used to walk virtually every day from downtown Monticello to his home on West Broadway, and virtually every day his walk included a stop at West End Service Station, where a seat was always reserved for him. There, a six-year-old boy would always observe him with awe, and the venerable judge would always take time to greet the boy and talk with him briefly.

Judge George L. Cooke died on September 3, 1959, and the boy he used to greet so graciously is grown now. I've met other lawyers and judges over the years, but in my mind I still define justice with the indelible image of George L. Cooke, and I always will. A more apt and accurate definition does not exist.

Judith Smith Kaye

MARIO CUOMO'S SELECTION of Judge Judith Kaye as chief judge of the New York State Court of Appeals has had the local press working overtime, digging up stories of her childhood in Monticello and comparing her with another distinguished chief judge from Monticello, Lawrence H. Cooke.

The comparisons between Judges Kaye and Cooke are inevitable. After all, the two have more in common than just their home town. One Albany newspaper suggested that Kaye will help restore the prestige the Court of Appeals enjoyed under Cooke, and then lost under his successor. She brings many of the same qualities to the bench that Cooke possessed.

But lost in all the comparisons is the fact that Sullivan County has provided the state with two other Court of Appeals judges, one of whom served as chief judge—quite a feat for a small rural county known mostly for its hotels?

Judge Sydney F. Foster, of Liberty, was a member of the Court of Appeals from 1960 until his retirement in 1963. But Judge Foster was not the first Sullivan County jurist to reach the state's highest court. That distinction belongs to Judge William B. Wright of Monticello, who was elected to the Court of Appeals in 1861, and was the chief judge at the time of his death in 1868.

Ironically, it was Judge Cooke who pointed out Judge Wright's accomplishments to me after Cooke had been called by yet another reporter asking about Kaye. "It's all right there in Quinlan's history," he said. "William B. Wright, a Monticello lawyer, eventually became chief judge of the Court of Appeals."

PERSONALITIES AND EVENTS

And so it is, right there in James Eldridge Quinlan's *History of Sullivan County*, published in 1873:

> He was of Irish blood, the son of Samuel and Martha Brown Wright, and was born in Newburgh, New York on the 16th of April, 1806. In April 1835, Mr. Wright opened a law office in Monticello, in the building now occupied for the same purpose by Judge Bush. At that time, Randall S. Street, Archibald C. Niven, Peter F. Hunn, Seth W. Brownson, and William B. Wright were the only lawyers in Monticello. Indeed, there was only one other in the county, Alpheus Dimmick of Bloomingburgh.

Quinlan goes on to recount Judge Wright's political career: elected to the New York State Assembly as the Whig candidate in 1846, elected to the state Supreme Court in 1847, and again in 1849 and 1857. "In 1861, he was nominated by the Republican Party for Judge of the Court of Appeals, and was elected. He served in that capacity until the January term of 1868, when he died. At the time of his decease, he was the Chief or Presiding Judge of the court." (At that time, "the judge of the Court of Appeals elected by the electors of the State, who shall have the shortest time to serve, shall be the chief judge of said court.")

Although not held in the high esteem Judge Lawrence Cooke has been accorded—many experts rate Cooke among the greatest chief judges of all time—Judge Wright was nonetheless a respected jurist. Upon his death, Ward Hunt, who succeeded him, declared that "his enduring monument will be found in the reports of the decisions of this court. Patient, laborious, learned, clear-minded, and discriminating, he ranks honorably in that long line of distinguished men who have presided on this bench."

Judge William B. Wright lived in Monticello for the better part of his life, and most of his judicial experience was obtained here. That makes Judge Judith Kaye Monticello's *third* chief judge of the state's highest court.

Chapter Two

Places of Interest

Readers are Last Resort in Search for First

ISAAC "YITS" KANTROWITZ was smiling broadly, an obvious look of satisfaction on his face. "Do you know the answer or not?" he asked me again, and I had to admit that I did not.

We had been discussing what life had been like in the village of Woodridge in the 1940s, and Yits had just finished an interesting story about growing up at a small hotel. He paused for a moment and then casually said, "I wonder how it all started, you know, where the first resort hotel in the county was located and when it was built." At first I thought he meant it rhetorically; he didn't seem to be demanding an answer. Then, almost as if he suddenly realized what he had asked, and that I hadn't replied, he wanted me to either answer the question or admit that I didn't know. Getting me to admit that I don't know something is very important to Yits.

I tried to explain that there wasn't much recorded about the earliest hotels, at least nothing authoritative. I said I had once read that the first summer hotel had been built in White Lake in 1811 by a Dr. Lindsley, but I wasn't sure of the accuracy of that report. Besides, I told him, one had to distinguish between the *business* hotels and the *resort* hotels, which catered almost exclusively to summer tourists. Surely the business hotels predated the resorts. Yits wasn't satisfied with that, and urged me to find out more.

Manville Wakefield wrote in *To the Mountains By Rail* that the first hotel for summer boarders was built by James B. Finlay in White Lake in 1845. That hotel, according to Wakefield, was run by Simeon M. Jordan, George B. Wooldridge, and Stephen Sweet. But Wakefield apparently got his information on the subject from *Child's Gazetteer*

PLACES OF INTEREST

of 1872-73, which quotes the Reverend J. B. Williams, then pastor of the Reformed Presbyterian Church at White Lake: "In the year 1846, Mr. Finlay built the first hotel for summer boarders. It was kept by Simon [*sic*] M. Jordan, George B. Wooldridge, Stephen Sweet, and others."

James Eldridge Quinlan, in his *History of Sullivan County*, concurs with the 1846 date. However, A. M. Scriber, a long-time editor of the *Republican Watchman*, who attempted to put together a history of the county himself in the 1930s, made mention of an earlier hotel in the January 12, 1940, issue of the paper. "An obscure note that 'William Gillespie in 1811 erected a storehouse on the turnpike near White Lake, and as considerable travel had commenced by this time, a hotel was opened and kept by Dr. Lindsley' may point to the first summer hotel in this region now noted chiefly for its summer hotel business," Scriber wrote. There is no further documentation of the Scriber claim. He does not mention where he found this "note" or on what authority it was made.

There was a Dr. John Lindsley in White Lake in the early 1800s—he was, in fact, the first physician in the town of Bethel—but I have found no record other than Scriber's claim that he ever ran a hotel. William Brown is usually credited with opening the first hotel in Bethel, sometime between 1800 and 1810.

It is known that there were hotels in the region before 1845, though they wouldn't be considered summer or resort hotels per se. The Mansion House in Monticello, for instance, was first opened in 1809 by David Hammond. It burned in 1871, was rebuilt shortly thereafter, and is still operating as the Monticello Inn. The Mansion House is a perfect example of a business hotel, and wouldn't come under consideration as the first summer hotel.

One man I met had a strong opinion about the issue. He had never spoken to me before, and I had no reason to believe he knew who I was. In fact, when he approached, I assumed it was to speak with someone else standing nearby. "As near as I can figure, the first summer hotel in the county was the Lake House in White Lake," he said, and that was it. No greeting, no introduction; just a simple declarative sentence.

RETROSPECT

We were standing in the middle of a small gathering of people, socializing after a meeting of the Sullivan County Historical Society at the county museum in Hurleyville.

His name was Jack Van Wert, he had worked as an automobile mechanic, and he lived in Smallwood, but that's about all I knew about him. I had seen him at historical society meetings before, but we had never spoken. He appeared to be in his 70s, but he spoke with an energy and enthusiasm that belied his age. He had obviously read about my attempt to pinpoint the year the first resort hotel began operating in Sullivan County. This was apparently his way of settling the dispute. In his mind, at least, there was no question.

"Yep, I believe that what was called the Lake House was the fist," he continued before I had a chance to say anything, nodding vigorously as he spoke. "I think you'll find I'm correct about that." He paused, and took a sip of coffee, seemingly awaiting a reply.

"What year was it built?" I asked.

"I'd say it must have been about 1845 or so," he said.

"I've seen a lot of conflicting information on the subject," I reminded him.

"Well, I'm quite certain that what they called the Lake House was the first hotel in White Lake, and there's no doubt that White Lake was the first resort," he said. "I've lived in that area all my life. It was really something when I was a kid, and North White Lake—that's what they call Kauneonga Lake today—was even more so. I'm telling you, in the summertime you couldn't even walk through the little square in the center of town, let alone drive a car through there. People were everywhere. And the lake itself—it wasn't unusual to see what, a thousand boats or more out there on a given afternoon, right on into evening. No powerboats back then, just rowboats and canoes and so on. It was quite a place, lots of hotels and casinos and summer homes. I don't think I'll ever forget it."

He paused to take another drink of his coffee. Then he turned to the tall, well-tanned man who had walked up a few moments before, and who had been standing there quietly, listening to our discussion. "Cy grew up in White Lake, too," he said, motioning to Cy Plotkin of Monticello. "In fact, he's got lots of photographs of the old hotels there."

PLACES OF INTEREST

Cy Plotkin nodded. I knew he was an accomplished amateur photographer, but I hadn't been aware of his interest in the old hotels.

"There were 30 hotels in and around White Lake at one point," Plotkin said. "I guess I've got most of them on film. Probably some of my photographs are the only ones that exist of some of the places."

"He's talking about hotels like the Kenmore, the Mansion House, the New Empire," Van Wert said. "You're probably too young to remember most of them, but between us, we've got pictures of 'em all."

"I've put together a slide show of the White Lake hotels," Plotkin said. "In fact, I think I might show it at a meeting of the historical society. Just this morning, they asked me to put on a program for one of our meetings. I said I would, but I didn't know what I'd do; now I believe I'll do the slide show. I've shown it other places, but never to the society. It's always received a good response, and I think people here will enjoy it."

"I know they will," Van Wert added. "I'll even help you with it; it'll be great. . ."

Crude Oil

A WEEK RARELY PASSES that I don't learn something new and interesting about Sullivan County, and usually it's quite by accident. Although it seems highly improbable today, there was once a significant link between Sullivan County and our nation's oil supply. That is, quite literally, *a link*. An obscure reference in Charles S. Hick's 1951 history of the town of Fremont leaves little doubt that a crude-oil pipeline once crossed that part of the county.

The iron pipeline, four to six inches in diameter, stretched overland from Olean, in upstate New York, to Bayonne, New Jersey. It was constructed to transport crude from the oil fields of western New York and Pennsylvania to the refineries of New Jersey. Hick estimated the line was built "sometime between 1870 and 1880," and since no mention is made of any pipeline in either Quinlan's *History of Sullivan County* or Child's *Gazetteer of Sullivan County*, both of which were published in 1873, one might assume that the pipe was laid after that date. The pipeline was owned by Standard Oil, John

RETROSPECT

D. Rockefeller's conglomerate, and operated under the auspices of the New York Transit Company.

"The pipeline that crossed Fremont was only a part of a big stretch," Hick wrote. "Powerful pumping stations were located along the line to force the oil through the pipes over the mountains. One of these was at Hancock, now converted into a woodworking plant. Another near Cochecton is in ruins."

Hick pointed out that a telegraph line ran along the same route for the entire length of the pipeline, and men were assigned to constantly walk the route, searching for leaks. If one was located, the telegraph line could be used to wire for a repair crew. This was an especially difficult task, given the rugged terrain throughout much of the town.

Of course, the construction technology of the day and the topography of that part of the county made frequent breaks in the line inevitable. Hick said residue from some of those leaks was still apparent years later. "West of Mileses on the hill the stream all the way to the Delaware River was once coated with crude oil," he wrote. "This killed the fish in the stream and the State Conservation Commission compelled the cleaning up of the stream. This was done by a crew working with brooms."

Hick estimated that "millions and millions" of barrels of crude oil must have passed through Fremont during the "50 or 60 year" operation of the pipeline, although he admits that it's hard to tell.

My wife Debbie told me that she had seen a reference to the pipeline in "The Cochecton Papers," published by the Town of Cochecton Bicentennial Committee in 1977. The book contained information about the pipeline after it had been taken over by the Columbia Gas System for natural gas transmission in 1927, though it did include photographs of the old pump station. And, town of Bethel historian Bert Feldman reminded me, "There is still a Pump Station Road in Cochecton."

Town of Delaware historian Mary Curtis had accumulated considerable information on the pipeline, including a 1979 article from *Upper Delaware* magazine which includes the recollections of William R. McDermott, whose father at one time ran the oil pumping station. "The ruins of a large brick building stand amid second-growth trees along Route 97 in Cochecton at the junction of that highway with

PLACES OF INTEREST

the Lake Huntington Road," the article begins. "The building is still known as 'the old oil pumping station' but nearly everyone has forgotten how important the station once was, and hardly anyone knows that the route of the old oil lines running from Bayonne, N.J. west is now the route of natural gas lines."

The pump stations were thirty miles apart, and it took a line walker three days to traverse the distance. The pump station in Cochecton was actually a series of buildings, including a pump house, boiler house, coal house, manifold building and telegraph office. The chimney on the boiler house was over 100 feet tall.

McDermott pointed out that the pumping station was abandoned in 1925, and the machinery and boiler were removed and the building knocked down. "The bricks from the boiler house and smokestack were laid up with lime and were reclaimed," he wrote. "The bricks from the pump house were laid up with cement and could not be reclaimed. That is why parts of the pump house can still be seen in the bushes along Route 97."

The crude oil of New York and Pennsylvania was paraffin-based, not the asphaltic-base of Texas and other continental shelf oil, and this made it a prized commodity in the manufacture of gasoline and motor oil for many years. Oil companies built their reputation on "pure Pennsylvania crude oil," and fortunes were made with it. None of it would have been possible without the Sullivan County "link."

For decades this strange monstrosity of a pipe was an incongruous but integral part of life in one of the county's most beautiful and undeveloped towns. Charles S. Hick recognized that, and made note of it. "No history of Fremont would be complete without a mention of the pipeline," he wrote.

Excelsior

NEWEIDEN, or Swamp Mills, as it was first known, once contained as much industry as any area of Sullivan County, and yet you are forgiven if you are not familiar with the place.

Swamp Mills, on the east branch of the Ten Mile River in the town of Tusten, was the site of that town's first town meeting in 1853. It was granted a post office in 1873. A few years later, a movement to find a more suitable name for the community was started, and many names, including Laurel Glen, were suggested. Each was rejected for one reason or another by the post office department.

Finally, in 1904, the names of two of the most prominent families in the area—Neumann and Weiden—were combined to come up with Neweiden, a name the post office department finally approved.

At one time, the tiny community included a sawmill, a brick yard, a blasting powder factory and an excelsior, or wood shaving, manufacturing mill. Of these, the excelsior mill is the most interesting for a number of reasons, not the least of which is that it is still standing. It looks very much as it did before the turn of the century, when it turned out four or five tons of shaved poplar a day.

Neweiden Excelsior Mill. Built in the late 19th century, the excelsior mill was operated into the 1930s, and looks today very much as it did when operations ceased. (Photo by Paul Gerry)

"It's as if it is frozen in time," says Robert Weiden, whose father last ran the mill in the 1930s. "Everything you see here is exactly as it was when the last bale was produced sixty years ago." That includes the dam on the Ten Mile River, which supplied the water power to run the turbine that operated the mill. Originally constructed of stone, the dam was reinforced with concrete by Weiden's father, and is still functional. So is much of the machinery in the mill—a circular saw, used for cutting bolts of fifty-four-inch-long wood into shorter billets, a series of eight shaving devices for turning the billets into shavings, and the compression baler, used to tightly pack the finished product into two-by-four-foot bales for storage and shipping.

"The excelsior could be turned out in a number of different grades of coarseness," Weiden explained. "It all depended on the use to which it would be put. Excelsior was used in packing, for filling upholstery for furniture, and for lining the bottom of caskets."

The foundation of the up-and-down sawmill—which probably dates back to about 1840—is also still well preserved, just downstream from the excelsior mill, though there is no longer any evidence of a structure there.

The Jupiter Powder Company is believed to have been started around 1870, when the bluestone quarrying industry was getting started along the Delaware River. The powder was indispensable to the quarrying business, and Jupiter Powder was produced until the plant was destroyed by fire in 1888.

The brick yard also thrived in the 1870s, although it is believed that this business didn't last very long. "I occasionally come across places in the woods where large amounts of clay were dug out for use in making the bricks," Weiden says. "But I don't think the bricks they produced were very good." Nonetheless, an 1874 advertisement proclaimed "Hard Bricks of superior quality and color for sale very cheap at the brick yards at Swamp Mills."

Weiden points out that much of the industry that grew up in the area was the brainchild of Augustus Lachenmeyer, a German immigrant who came to Sullivan County in 1867. Weiden has discovered that Lachenmeyer was a multi-talented fellow. "He holds several patents used at one time in the brewing industry, and he patented the kind of hand-held pencil sharpener school kids used to use. He was also a linguist and a musician." Lachenmeyer operated the business until around 1885, when he returned to Germany.

Weiden's grandfather, who was in the furniture business in New York City, purchased the mill in 1904. The Weiden family still owns the mill and much of the surrounding property, although they all live elsewhere. "My brothers and I would like to see the mill preserved as much as possible," Weiden says. "We think it has some real historic value."

RETROSPECT

Residents Resisted Tuberculosis Retreats

IT IS COMMON KNOWLEDGE that Sullivan County, and the Liberty area in particular, was once a haven for patients with tuberculosis. But just how much impact the sanitoriums established for the treatment of the dread pulmonary infection had on the county is far less well known.

The controversy over whether or not the county should ban sanitoriums, such as the one begun at Loomis in 1896, reached a fever pitch just after the turn of the century, and a growing concern over the spread of germs took on increasingly ludicrous overtones, perhaps best illustrated by the fly-swatting contest sponsored by the *Liberty Register* newspaper in 1912.

Sullivan County's reputation as a haven for tubercular patients actually began before the Loomis Sanitorium opened just outside the village of Liberty. Dr. Alfred L. Loomis, of New York City, was stricken with the disease and sought relief at the cottage of a Liberty physician, Dr. Edward L. Trudeau, where he spent six months recuperating.

Realizing that a tubercular patient, or consumptive, as they were known at the time, could recover nicely in the mountain air—at a time when nearly all doctors were recommending warmer climates to those with the disease—Loomis decided to open his own sanitorium. He purchased land atop a hill on the road to White Sulphur Springs, and through the generosity of some of his wealthy patients (notably J. Pierpont Morgan, who donated $60,000), the Loomis Sanitorium was officially opened in 1896.

Dr. Loomis never realized his dream, however—he died shortly before it opened. His sister-in-law, Mrs. Richard Irvin, was appointed the sanitorium's first president.

The facility—the county's most famous, and one of the nation's most successful—eventually occupied some 700 acres and employed more than 100 workers. When fire severely damaged the complex in 1899, destroying its generator and leaving it without electric lights, Morgan again came to the rescue by purchasing the entire plant of the Liberty Light and Power Company and presenting it as a gift to the sanitorium, which in turn sold power back to the village.

Soon, advertisements were appearing in publications throughout the country touting Catskill Mountain air as a cure for consumptives. Other facilities, albeit smaller, began operating in and around Liberty, and the Ontario and Western Railroad got into the act in 1896, publishing a booklet dedicated to advertising such facilities.

But not everyone in Sullivan County was happy with the success of the sanitoriums. Letters to the editors of local newspapers, criticizing the influx of patients to the area, began appearing in 1902. Sullivan County's summer tourist trade had already been dealt a devastating blow by the new reputation it was developing, opponents maintained, and county residents "must now choose whether they want a health resort or a pleasure resort," the letters claimed. The town of Callicoon banned sanitoriums in 1913, and in 1918, the village of Liberty, responding to public panic over the spreading of germs, began enforcing an ordinance against spitting in public.

But the *Liberty Register* "Swat the Fly" contest in July 1912 seemed to best illustrate the futility of the opposition. Although the paper reported that some 114,481 flies were killed in an effort to halt the spread of disease, the contest drew only a half dozen contestants.

Despite the outcry, the Loomis sanitorium continued to survive, if not to thrive. By the 1930s, however, it was forced to increasingly curtail its services. In 1933, some of the outlying buildings were closed; in 1936, a number of unused cottages were turned over to the Fresh Air Fund of the New York *Herald Tribune*. In 1938, its operating funds dwindling rapidly, Loomis cut its staff by about forty members, and reduced activities by roughly a third. Loomis closed in 1943.

The dread of tuberculosis would shortly fade, and with it the sanitoriums which once helped put Sullivan County on the medical map, much to the chagrin of many of its residents.

RETROSPECT

Monticello Industries in the Early 1900s

MOST OF US are aware of the magnitude and the importance of the tanning industry in Sullivan County in the early and mid-1800s, and one of the largest factories in the county during that time was located in Monticello, but there was other noteworthy industry as well. Long after the tanning industry had faded from the scene, the village of Monticello remained the home of thriving factories with significant payrolls.

One of the most unusual and prosperous factories in the village was Joseph Engelmann's cigar factory, located on Mill Street, which has since become St. John Street.

Engelmann came to Monticello from Narrowsburg in the early 1890s. In addition to the cigar factory, he ran a sleigh and harness store on Fulton Street, and also served as president (mayor) of the village for a time. It was the cigar factory, though, for which he was best known.

The factory was located on the corner of Mill Street and what is currently Roosevelt Place. The building itself was designed to resemble a private residence more than an industrial plant. In his historical recollection *Old Monticello*, Edward F. Curley described the structure as having the appearance of "a select residential home."

"With its beautiful green lawns, the climbing rose bushes, the many, many flower beds of great beauty, combined with the artistic building, it was a magnificent property," Curley wrote.

The cigar factory produced two brands of hand-rolled Havana cigars: the County Seat and the Engelmann Special. It is said that sales of the two brands combined to surpassed the two million mark in 1898. The factory employed a number of men, the most famous of whom was its supervising foreman, Isaac Levens, better known throughout the county as "Johnnie Smoker." Curley says Levens was a popular figure at the hotels and restaurants in the county, as he made the rounds promoting the Engelmann cigars.

"'Johnnie' was possessed with a musical voice, and not being of a bashful disposition, he was always ready and willing to render his musical talents to those desiring them," Curley wrote. "It was his

PLACES OF INTEREST

delight to entertain the jury men who would attend the various courts during the year, with his songs and witty sayings. It is needless to say that many a housewife throughout the county has heard the name of 'Johnnie Smoker' spoken of by their husbands after returning from Sullivan County jury duty."

The company also employed two traveling salesmen, identified by Curley as Charles Lang and Louis Weed. In addition, Curley lists the other employees as John Botens, John Hessling, Edwin Gebhardt, Frank Reiser, August Botens, Nick Knorr, Charles Rosenfelder, Charles Snyder, Albert Schmidt, Henry and Frank Robinson, Jack and Willie Parks, Louis Helm, Louis Flanders, Frank Davis, Sadie and Bertha Hix, John Avery, William Hindley, and Mollie Bedford.

Curley says the cigar factory payroll was substantial, and contributed significantly to the economy of the village. "Saturday noon each week was payday, and most of the money received by these employees would be spent within our village." Of course, that wasn't at all unusual in those days, when most people spent their entire lives within one community. Shopping trips to elsewhere in the county, or to Middletown, for instance, were unheard of.

Joseph Engelmann's cigar factory was one of the most successful and unusual factories in the village in the early 1900s, but it wasn't the only one. In fact, the Chant glove factory, which was a viable enterprise for a number of years, was built adjacent to the cigar factory on Mill Street.

Virtually everyone who lived in Monticello at the time knew the factory as the Chant Glove Factory, because it was under the supervision of Miss Chant. (In fact, Curley referred to the factory as the Chant Factory.)

The Kayser Company operated a number of plants throughout the country, including one in Brooklyn, and for a few years, a second plant in Monticello. This second plant opened in 1917 under the supervision of Frances McNeeley. The two factories employed a total of 128 women in 1918, and in 1919 their combined weekly payroll was over $1,100, a sum the *Republican Watchman* called "a nice amount of money to come into Monticello every week to spend among the business houses and amusement places."

In fact, the *Watchman* devoted a front page story on March 21, 1919, to the bonuses the women at the two glove factories would receive that year. The Kayser Company apparently paid its workers bonuses based on their time of service and the amount of work they had turned out the previous year. In 1918, the company paid out over $1,100 in bonuses in the form of War Savings Stamps. Under a revised formula, the bonuses in 1919 were considerably higher, and were paid in cash. In some cases, these bonuses were said to amount to as much as $100 per woman. According to the *Watchman* article, those workers employed by Kayser for seven years or more received bonuses equivalent to 7.5 percent of the work they had produced the year before; those women with two years employment were eligible for 2 percent bonuses.

The *Watchman* called the two Monticello plants among the most productive of the Kayser group. The article stated, "The Kayser Company is very much pleased with the Monticello factories' work both in quality and volume, and Miss Chant and Miss McNeeley have received many deserved compliments."

An employees' strike at some of the other Kayser plants in the spring of 1919 made the two Monticello plants even more valuable, the *Watchman* pointed out: "During the last few days, the Monticello factories have been operating on surplus work because of a strike in the Brooklyn factories and other factories throughout the country. The strike started several days ago through the efforts of agitators because of a change in the management."

It is not clear exactly when or why the Kayser Glove factories in Monticello closed down. Curley makes no mention of the closings in his book, and of course, newspaper files from back then are scarce. It is known that the glove factories were among the last industrial operations in the village of Monticello. With the passing of these plants came the passing of an era in which the resort industry existed in harmony with other light industry in the county.

Of course, other industries came around later, including one, to my chagrin, I had never heard about. Monticello Industries, a division of Noma Electric Company, specialized in the manufacture of Christmas tree lights. With the onset of World War II, the solder necessary for the manufacture of those lights became difficult to obtain, and the company went looking for another line of work. That search led Noma to Monticello and to the manufacture of toy trucks.

PLACES OF INTEREST

There were three plants in the village: two on Broadway—one next to St. Peter's Church and another where Rhulen Insurance was later located—and one in the parish house at St. John's Church. In addition, the company utilized about ten garages as warehouses. At its peak, the operation employed some 170 persons in Monticello, including Ida Rodels as office manager and Eleanor Davis as bookkeeper.

"Lots of people from around town worked there," Rodels said. "They ranged in age from sixteen to ninety—that's right, we had one gentleman working for us who was ninety years old. He was everyone's favorite employee, too."

"And you made toy trucks?" I asked. "What exactly did that entail?"

"They were wooden trucks," she said. "We used to buy wood moldings from someone in Claryville; that was the only kind of wood we could use. We had just two customers—Sears Roebuck and Montgomery Ward—but they bought an awful lot of trucks."

"What did these toy trucks look like?" I asked. "Is it possible I used to have one?"

"They were cute little things, about this long," she said, holding her hands about ten inches apart. "We used to do everything. We built them, painted them and packaged them. They had movable wheels and a few other separate pieces, though they never seemed very sturdy. We used to joke that the minute some kid would get hold of them they'd fall apart, but they must have been good; we sold thousands of them. I believe we shipped out about 200 cartons a day. After the war was over, the owners wanted to build a factory for something like $4 million next to the O&W Station on St. John Street, but I guess they couldn't get any kind of favorable tax deal from the village, so they moved the whole operation to Middletown."

"You mean the village didn't want them?" I asked.

"I'm not really sure why they left Monticello," Eleanor Davis said. "But after the war they built a factory in Middletown which employed about 400 people. I worked with them there for a few years, myself."

The caliber of the work force available in Sullivan County is often cited as a reason why more industry doesn't locate here, but it didn't hurt the toy factory. For instance, neither of the women knew anything about the toy business when they were hired, but that didn't affect their work. "The woman who interviewed me asked me what made me think I could run a toy factory," Ida remembers. "I told her an office is an office and a set of books is a set of books. I guess that was the right answer, because she hired me."

Both women agreed that the company's owners, Sedaka and Rothchild, were pleasant men who were easy to work for. "It was a very interesting job," Eleanor Davis said. "I enjoyed working there."

"I'll never forget the years I worked there," Ida Rodels added, a bit misty-eyed. "In fact, to this day, every time I see a toy truck I think of it."

Fancy Glass

DECORATIVE PUNCH BOWLS, fancy salt and pepper shakers, and the finest etched stemware, direct from Sullivan County. That's right: Some of the most elaborate and best crafted glass on the market once came from the Barryville Cut Glass Shop.

The Barryville Cut Glass Shop was built about 1910 on Halfway Brook, which provided the power for its cutting and polishing wheels. In fact, if you look closely at the brook just before Route 55 intersects Route 97 in Barryville, the falls and the foundation from the glass factory are still clearly visible.

Barryville Cut Glass Factory. Located on Halfway Brook, it once produced fancy etched glass for Libbey. (Author's colleciton)

The glass shop was built and originally operated by William Henry Gibbs, who also owned a similar, larger plant in Hawley, Pennsylvania. Gibbs was born in Indian Orchard, just outside Honesdale, and learned the glass-cutting trade at the mammoth plant in White Mills, Pennsylvania, where he began working in 1882. From White Mills, Gibbs went to New York City, Pittsburgh, Wheeling,

PLACES OF INTEREST

Toledo, and Corning, perfecting his craft. He opened his own plant in Honesdale in 1895, in partnership with Michael J. Kelly. This successful plant turned out intricately cut glass the equal of any on the market at the time, and at its peak employed about thirty people.

Gibbs later formed a partnership with William G. Sell, and in 1909 moved his operation to Hawley, a few miles away. In 1910, he built the Barryville enterprise, and in 1911 located one in Stroudsburg, Pennsylvania, as well. The two-story wooden building in Barryville was home to about fifteen workers from 1910 to about 1920. The Libbey Glass Company supplied the blanks for etching. Gibbs sold the Barryville plant to the Krantz & Sell Company in 1912.

Highland Town Historian Austin Smith, whose father, Edward, was employed at the glass shop, remembers the plant when it was operational. "The plant was run by a turbine, water-powered, of course," Smith recalls. "And that meant it was dependent on the water level of Halfway Brook, and that varied quite a bit, depending on the weather and the time of year. One day, the plant manager comes to the workers and tells them that because the water level of the brook had dropped so low, they were all going to be laid off until it rained enough to raise the stream.

"Needless to say, that didn't set too well with the boys, so they got the idea that they could go up to Highland Lake, where Halfway Brook originates, and take a couple of boards off the dam, to let more water over it. That raised the brook up enough that the plant could operate even without the rain. By the time the plant manager figured out what had happened, it was too late to do anything about it."

Smith compiled a considerable amount of history of the plant over the years, and counts among his collection a piece of the etched glass manufactured there. "People tend to forget that this whole area was a center of cut glass manufacturing back then," Smith says. "The Barryville plant was small, of course, but look it up, there were plants in Hawley and Honesdale, and the most famous one of them all, in White Mills." The White Mills plant, Smith points out, employed some 650 people at its peak, and turned out the world-famous Dorflinger glass beginning in the 1870s.

Although the Barryville plant never approached the renown of its competition across the river, William Henry Gibbs was as skilled a craftsman who ever etched a glass, and the products of his plant are still highly regarded by collectors. Besides, the waterfalls and foundation that remain on Halfway Brook in Barryville make for interesting conversation.

The Saga of the Delaware Ferry

SOMETIMES the more we find out about a particular subject the more we realize how much we don't know. For several months my wife Debbie and I had been pausing on our daily walks along the Delaware River in Barryville to speculate about a peculiar stone-and-mortar tower on the riverbank not far from our house. Neither of us was sure what the structure had once been, nor how old it was. Our initial guess was that it was in some way connected with the Delaware & Hudson Canal, but we both agreed that the route of the canal didn't run that close to the river in that immediate area.

One day we noticed the remnants of what looked like a similar structure on the bank on the opposite side. This provided us with the

Sholoa-Barryville Bridge. Originally constructed in 1856, the piers from this suspension bridge are still prominent on the banks of the Delaware River and were mistaken by the author for the remains of a ferry tow. (Author's collection)

first real clue to the function of the structure on our side. I pointed out to Debbie that this new discovery, along with the fact that we had previously noticed what looked like the remains of cable in the structure on our side of the river, led me to believe that the towers were once part of some sort of cable-drawn ferry system.

"I'm quite sure that there was once a ferry across the Delaware in this general vicinity," I told her, vaguely recalling a map of turn-of-the-century Barryville I had once seen. "This could well have been part of it." Debbie didn't disagree, but she insisted that we try to find out more about the two structures. "I'd like to know for sure what they used to be," she kept telling me. So, at her urging, we looked up Austin Smith.

Smith, the town of Highland historian, has lived in Barryville all of his life, and has accumulated considerable knowledge about the area. We had spoken with him on previous occasions when we needed to know something and had nowhere else to turn, and he had always provided us with the information we sought. He seemed genuinely happy to hear from us again, and invited us over to his house to look at some old photographs he said might shed some light on our query.

"I've been giving some thought to your question," he said upon greeting us at his back door. "I'm not entirely sure about the ferry, but I have no doubt about those stone towers you're wondering about." Smith led us into his kitchen, and we sat down at the table. He immediately surrounded us with stacks of books and photographs.

He explained that he hadn't at first made the connection when we asked about the towers, but after realizing what it was we were asking about, had little difficulty clearing up the question. "You are, of course, familiar with the bridge that crosses the river into Shohola right down here," he said, pointing just down Route 97. "Well, that bridge used to be upriver a ways, off River Road. Those towers were the supports for that bridge."

Smith produced a copy of a photograph similar to the one I had recalled seeing. He pointed out the bridge on it. "There were two different suspension bridges there," he said. "They both collapsed, and were finally replaced by the present-day bridge."

I pointed to a spot just down river from where the bridge had once been. There were dotted lines across the river, and the word "ferry" between them. "That's the ferry I was thinking of," I said. I could see from the photo that it was downriver from the old bridge, about halfway between it and the present span.

"That's right," Smith agreed. "And I'd say you're going to want to do some more investigating along the river bank."

"Why's that?" I asked.

"Because it looks to me like the ferry run was located just about where your house is now." Smith produced dozens of photographs of 19th century Barryville, many of them covering the very section of the river on which I believe the ferry crossed, but none of them showing any traces of a ferry.

The only thing left to do, I decided, was to find some sort of physical evidence that the ferry really existed. I thought this might be possible because of the remnants of the suspension bridge that crossed the Delaware from Barryville to Shohola from 1856 to 1941. Even though the ferry probably predated that bridge, I thought that, if it was the cable-drawn type, perhaps some remnant of the anchors for the cable still remained.

I convinced my brother Joe to help me explore both sides of the riverbank. Although the maps I had seen had not been to scale, I had a fairly good idea of approximately where the ferry was located—I had narrowed it down to a quarter-mile stretch. On a chilly Sunday morning we climbed down from River Road to the river. Huge chunks of ice were randomly deposited along the shore, reminders of the frigid winter. Thick underbrush and miscellaneous debris not only made walking difficult but made the prospect of uncovering anything useful unlikely.

"What exactly do you hope to find?" my brother asked me when we reached river level. I didn't really know, but I reasoned that if some sort of anchors still existed, we'd recognize them if we saw them.

The bank sloped up about fifteen feet toward River Road, which ran parallel to the river. Along most of the bank a neatly laid-up stone wall supported the roadway. "Somewhere in here, I think we might find some stonework which served as an anchor for the cable," I said as we walked, but Joe seemed increasingly skeptical.

We searched for roughly an hour, looking carefully along the base of the stone wall. Finally, not far from the abutment of the old suspension bridge, we discovered two concrete pedestals, about two feet square and three feet high. I thought they might be exactly what we'd been looking for. "They're too close to the bridge," Joe said, still the skeptic. "Besides, they're concrete. If the ferry did pre-date the bridge, chances are the anchors would be made of some sort of stone and mortar, like the bridge abutments."

Still, I excitedly took news of my discovery to Austin Smith. He had been, at first, skeptical about the ferry. In fact, he told me point blank on our first meeting that he had never heard of the ferry and doubted that one had ever run between Barryville and Shohola. "Wasn't needed," he maintained, "you could walk across the river if you had to." Little by little, I managed to convince him that there probably had been a ferry. "Had to be," he reasoned. "How else would they have got logs or stone or whatever to the railroad before the bridge was built in 1856?"

He was seated at his kitchen table when I told him of my newest discovery, describing the pedestals as best I could. he just smiled, reached behind him for a book, and turned a few pages. Silently, he pointed out a photograph. There, plainly visible just to the right of the old suspension bridge, were the two concrete bases—telephone poles extending from them.

Delaware Ferry. Surely a ferry of this type ran between Barryville and Shohola, Pa. at least from 1848 until 1856. (Author's collection)

RETROSPECT

"That's how they carried the wires across the river," Smith said, chuckling. "If you still hope to find that ferry, you'd better climb back down there before the river level rises any so there's no room to walk."

There were still many questions left to be answered. When did the ferry run? What type of ferry was it? Where exactly did it make its crossing?

Smith had become almost as interested in the subject as I was, and contacted me whenever he discovered something he considered relevant. Our most recent speculation had involved the type of ferry. Before the technology to build bridges across rivers of any significant width or depth developed, ferries served as the only means of getting groups of people or loads of material from one side to the other. Some early ferries were cable-drawn; some were powered by a team of horses running on a treadmill which turned a paddlewheel. Some ferries on the Hudson River, for example, used two teams of horses. One team would be used for crossing from east to west, then rested while the other team brought the boat back. On the last trip of the day, one team would have to swim back across the river behind the ferry.

I've not yet been able to determine what type of ferry was used to cross the Delaware River at Barryville in years gone by. If there was one, it was most probably a simple, cable-drawn system.

After exploring the river bank with me, my brother suggested the ferry was probably nothing more than a crude raft, positioned in such a way that the current alone would push it across from one side of the river to the other.

Smith, too, worked hard on the puzzle. One day he uncovered an old post card in excellent condition. I had seen many others like it in a scrapbook he had shown me, but I didn't recall this one. "Take a good look at that picture and tell me what you think," he said.

The card displayed a crude, raft-like boat, floating a horse-drawn wagon across a river. A cable was strung overhead, connected to the boat below by two slack lines. "It's a ferry," I said. "It's exactly the kind of ferry my brother had said probably crossed the Delaware."

Smith smiled. "And you see where it ran," he said.

PLACES OF INTEREST

The upper left corner of the postcard revealed that it was indeed a ferry, and that it had regularly crossed the Delaware River near Masthope, Pennsylvania, upstream from Barryville.

"Do you see how it worked?" Smith asked. "The river current carried it along, while the cable overhead guided it. Pointed in the right direction, it would cross the river without any other power."

"So you think if this type of ferry crossed the Delaware at Masthope, the same kind might have been used at Barryville?" I asked.

"Makes sense," he said. "Remember the map you showed me with the dotted lines indicating the ferry run? The lines ran diagonally across the river. If the ferry was powered by river current and nothing else, that's how it would have run—diagonally. I figured it all fits."

"Of course, it's not proof or anything," I conceded. "What we really need is a schedule or something, something no one can argue with."

"Now you're talking," he said, "You and your brother take another look along the riverbank. If there was a cable strung across there, there could be some kind of anchor left on shore. Meantime, I'll keep poking around for some sort of record."

It's not as if Smith is a particularly stubborn man or anything, it's just that he requires cold, hard evidence before he's willing to revise his version of Sullivan County history.

And that came just after my wife discovered a reference to the ferry in a book on canoeing the Delaware. "The book says the present bridge form Barryville to Shohola is built on the site of an old ferry crossing," she told me.

There it was, in black and white. It seemed to make sense—the bridge was just downstream from the point we had first estimated to be the location of the crossing. Smith seemed to take a renewed interest in the subject when I excitedly told him of the reference. "I suppose it's possible," he said. "There was a road which ran down to the river on the Pennsylvania side."

One of the criteria we had used in our efforts to determine the most likely site was access to the river from the road. There were only a few short stretches of the river in the vicinity of where the crossing could have been which offered that access. The site of the bridge was one. "Tell you what I'm going to do," Smith finally said after studying the book. "I'll take you down to the old road, and we'll walk along the river bank and see what we find."

Within a few days, Smith, my wife, my dog and I hiked down the old road to the river. We had spent considerable time studying the riverbank on the Barryville side, but had never before visited the Shohola side. Smith was a knowledgeable and articulate guide. On the way to the river, he pointed out the grave of Chauncey Thomas, the man who had built the old Barryville-Shohola suspension bridge just upstream, and an old cinder block factory that operated along the river bank.

Once we reached the river, both Smith and I came to the same conclusion. "If there was a ferry crossing here, and I'm not saying there was," he told me, "it would have had to have been upstream from this bridge. Otherwise, you're too close to the rapids." He was right: The present bridge was constructed just a few yards upriver of the rushing water of the Shohola Rapids. Had the ferry below the bridge strayed just a bit off course, it would have been washed downstream. "That's what they used to call Mitchie Falls," Smith pointed out. "It's unlikely they had a ferry crossing so close."

Nevertheless, we walked the bank for a hundred yards or so in both directions, searching for some evidence that a ferry once docked there. Just as we had so many times before, we found nothing. "Let's figure this thing out again," Smith said after we had abandoned the search. "Assuming for the moment that there was a ferry, we know from the one map we found which mentioned it that it was somewhere in this general vicinity." He motioned along a stretch of river as he spoke. "We know it had to be in an eddy, and not near any rapids, and we know there had to be access to the river from the road. Now we see that the bridge was built on the site of the crossing. Let's assume that means that it was built somewhere near the crossing. Where does that leave us?"

"I'd say right back where we started," I said. "The ferry crossed right by our house."

"It's like I told you before," Smith said, smiling that sly smile of his. "You've got to find some proof. Until you do, I still say there never was a ferry. But I sure do hope you'll keep trying to convince me otherwise. I really enjoy these little trips of ours."

PLACES OF INTEREST

Passenger Pigeons

THE PASSENGER PIGEON was once one of the most abundant birds in North America. James Audubon estimated flocks of passenger pigeons to exceed one *billion* birds. It is estimated that such a flock would consume over eight and a half million bushels of food a day. The beautiful red-breasted bird got its name from the fact that it was often traveling in search of new food supplies once those in a given area were depleted.

The last passenger pigeon in the wild is believed to have been killed just prior to the turn of the century. The last one in captivity died in the Cincinnati Zoological Gardens in 1914. Not a single passenger pigeon has been seen anywhere since.

In the late 1800s, however, the birds existed in such numbers in Sullivan County that it is almost unbelievable. It thrived on beechnuts—and what better place to find that food than the Livingston Manor area? The beechnut supply lasted longer than most, and if not for the commercial hunting of these birds, they might still inhabit the county.

The birds were so plentiful and were considered such a delicacy that a huge regional industry grew up around them. The passenger pigeon was slaughtered in large numbers and packed in barrels for shipment to New York City restaurants. Many of the early roads into the mountains in the DeBruce and Shin Creek areas were cut in order to facilitate the removal of large quantities of pigeons.

The method in which these birds were caught is considered by many to have given rise to the popular expression "stool pigeon." These birds traveled in such numbers that the sky was literally blackened when a flock passed overhead; some have estimated that a flock might take up an area of sky measuring one mile wide by 150 miles long. Obviously, the flock followed the leaders wherever they went.

With that in mind, commercial pigeon hunters in Livingston Manor built large nets baited with buckwheat to attract the birds, but had little success—the flock would be attracted to the food, all right, but would hover over the nets without coming close enough to be caught. Only a few birds were captured in this way.

RETROSPECT

Finally, the hunters tried a different approach. Realizing that the birds followed one another, they took a few captured pigeons and sewed their eyes shut (so the birds could smell food and would fly toward it without seeing the net). These birds were placed on long poles and held aloft near the nets. When a flock of pigeons approached, the hunters would shake the poles, jarring the pigeons off the perch, from where they would fly toward the food in the net. Many of the birds in the flock would follow, and were thus caught in the nets and later killed. The birds on the poles were called "stool pigeons."

Cruel as it was, pigeon hunting was once a major industry in Sullivan County. What impact local hunting had on the demise of the species is not known. What is known is that while the passenger pigeon thrived on the beechnuts of Sullivan County, the county's commerce thrived on the bird. It may never be known whether the beechnuts or the birds were exhausted first.

Memories of Majestic Mongaup Falls

IT ROSE MAJESTICALLY over eighty feet in the air, a steady stream of rushing water, and in the early 1900s it played host to thousands of spectators each year. It was Mongaup Falls, generally regarded as the third highest falls in the state of New York until its destruction at the hands of the Rockland Light & Power Company in 1922.

Mongaup Falls was located in the town of Forestburgh, about a mile and a half southwest of the center of the hamlet that shared that name. The Mongaup River was about fifty feet wide as it approached the falls, but narrowed suddenly to about fifteen feet just before plunging over the rocky precipice. Huge rock formations, ranging up to thirty feet high on either side, confined the stream to that width just above the falls, adding an incredible force to the cascading water.

The first drop of the falls was about twenty feet. At that point, the water formed a sort of whirlpool before falling three more times in quick succession. The water directly below the eighty-foot drop was extremely deep, and several holes, called "kettle holes" by old timers, were even deeper. An article in the October 28, 1938, edition of the *Republican Watchman* newspaper, recalling the heyday of the

PLACES OF INTEREST

falls, referred to logs caught in those kettle holes being ground to sharp points by the force of the water.

It hardly needs mention that Mongaup Falls was a favorite sightseeing spot, especially among picnickers. There were two popular vantage points. Just downstream from the falls, one could view the full height of the drop and witness firsthand the power of the descending water. One hundred feet above the falls was "flat rock," another popular viewing area. From this point, spectators were treated to a magnificent panorama of the scene.

But Mongaup Falls was much more than a tourist attraction. For many years it was one of the focal points of industry—of life—in Forestburgh. A large gang sawmill operated just below the falls for several years in the 1850s, and other mills, owned by men named Wheeler, Barnum, and Gilman, and tanneries, a quarry and a wheelbarrow factory, all drew on the power of the Mongaup River.

It all ended in 1922, when workmen from Rockland Power converged on the falls with rock drills and dynamite. What resulted was the Mongaup Reservoir, and the massive turbines that produced the electricity the corporation supplied to Port Jervis, Middletown, and beyond.

Though the drilling and blasting and building marked the falls for oblivion, its specter has proven more difficult to obliterate. For those of us not fortunate to have seen this magnificence of nature, there are recorded memories, though pale by comparison. Alfred B. Street, one of the most highly respected poets of his era, once wrote of Mongaup Falls:

> Struggling along the mountain path
> We hear amid the gloom
> Like a roused giant's voice of wrath
> A deep toned, sullen boom.
> Emerging on a platform high
> Burst sudden to the startled eye
> Rocks, woods and waters, wild and rude
> A scene of savage solitude.

Mongaup Falls was awe inspiring, and it has never been—indeed, can never be—replaced. Perhaps the article in the *Watchman* said it best:

Time marches on and they battered down the falls to make a power plant, but the strange beauty of [the] scene once there will long be remembered. The spot still has its appeal and many enjoy a visit to the region as it now stands, with the mighty lake held back to light cities and countryside and furnish power for more industry than the early settlers could dream would ever come to this part of the state... Sullivan County's mighty Mongaup Falls is harnessed and is no more. Its memory lingers.

Cowboys, Alligators and Renegade Bison

JUST LIKE MOST BOYS who grew up in the 1950s or early 1960s, my best friend Bob and I loved to play cowboy. We spent hours pretending to be the Lone Ranger, the Range Rider, Roy Rogers, or my own personal favorite, Hopalong Cassidy, slaying badmen and rescuing damsels in distress.

As much as Bob enjoyed playing cowboy, though, I was always just a bit more intense. I actually aspired to be a cowboy. I used to practice my fast draw against the many characters on television westerns, and my grandmother used to say she never saw me without a six-shooter strapped to my hip. What a thrill it was for me to visit amusement parks like Carson City and Ghost Town U.S.A. in upstate New York, and Wild West City in New Jersey. It was even more of a thrill when an honest-to-goodness wild west town opened up in Sullivan County.

It was called Cimarron City, and it occupied a large tract of land just off Quickway exit 106, east of Monticello. For someone like me, it presented more than just the opportunity to visit another amusement park with a western theme—it presented me with the prospect of pursuing my chosen profession close to home. I figured I would get a job as a cowboy at Cimarron City.

Unfortunately, that was not to be. Cimarron City lasted just a few summers, and at some point becoming a cowboy lost some of its appeal to me. Still, for years after its closing, the abandoned buildings of Cimarron City remained a fitting legacy of what had been. The

PLACES OF INTEREST

giant billboard with the cowboy waving his hat to passersby survived long after the last customer passed through the gate.

Joe Kraf of Mountaindale was one of five partners who owned Cimarron City. The idea for the park, he says, came from a friend of his who had opened Carson City in Catskill in the late 1950s, and had enjoyed great success there. "He was doing quite well up there," Kraf told me. "We figured we could do the same thing here. With the tourist season and all, we figured it would be a natural."

Kraf says the group invested about $300,000 in buildings and attractions. They anticipated needing about one hundred thousand customers a summer to break even. "We had about thirty buildings," he recalls. "There was a saloon, several shops, three restaurants. We averaged between 75,000 and 80,000 customers a summer for five or six years. After that we just couldn't afford to lose any more money."

Admission to the park was fifty cents for children and one dollar for adults. Some of the attractions, including the horse and pony rides, the stage ride, and the train ride, cost an additional twenty-five or thirty cents each. One of the unique and most popular attractions was the boat ride, featuring a paddlewheeler. "We bought the shell of a boat," Kraf says. "We did a lot of work on it to convert it to the riverboat we used at the park."

Cimarron City also featured a "genuine" Seminole Indian who wrestled alligators in a small pool just outside of town. "I'll never forget the day he arrived in town," Kraf says. "He drives up with this little enclosed trailer behind his car. Inside the trailer he has these two live alligators." Kraf supervised park personnel in building the pool for the alligator wrestler that same morning in order to have it ready for the afternoon opening.

Cimarron City also featured live entertainment: a wild west show depicting a stage coach hold-up and subsequent shoot-out. For this, they hired real cowboy actors. "We contacted some of the parks already in existence," Kraf remembers. "They helped us get in touch with someone who arranged the acts. We always felt we had a better attraction than any of the other parks. We just couldn't make it go. The weather was partly to blame, but maybe it was just a little ahead of its time. We certainly had some unique and novel attractions, and people still remember many of them."

RETROSPECT

Of all the fond memories I have of Cimarron City, one stands out from all the rest. I was riding with my mother into Monticello early one morning in 1964. We exited the Quickway at 106, and approached Cimarron City. There, in the middle of the road at six in the morning, was a woman being chased by a bison! My mother managed to maneuver the car in between the fleeing woman and the enraged bison, which had escaped from Cimarron City, and the woman was able to get into the car, shaken but unharmed.

That's the closest to being a cowboy hero that I ever got.

The Liberty Highway

A SLEEK, LUXURIOUS BMW is effortlessly negotiating the tortuous curves of a stretch of mountain highway when an oncoming truck blows a tire and swerves into the car's path. The driver deftly dodges disaster, demonstrating the agile handling of the "Bimmer." The scene is a familiar one; it was used on and off for more than two years as a BMW television commercial.

The road is the portion of Route 97 just over the Orange/Sullivan County line known as the Hawk's Nest.

The Hawk's Nest is one of America's truly great stretches of road, not only for its endless succession of curves, but for the jagged mountain cliffs on one side and the steep dropoff to the picturesque Delaware River on the other. It is also one of America's most filmed stretches of road. Besides the BMW commercial, the Hawk's Nest has been featured in ads for American Express, Porsche and Peugeot, among others. Although never actually identified in the ads, the unusual highway is easily recognizable.

Detail from Liberty Highway advertisement. This ad campaign by the White Motor Company put Sullivan County on the national map. (Sullivan County Republican)

PLACES OF INTEREST

As well known as the Hawk's Nest has become, it is far from the first area road to have gained such notoriety. The same distinction used to belong to a stretch of Old Route 17, or Route 4 as it was once labeled, which became known as the Liberty Highway. As has been the case with the Hawk's Nest, the Liberty Highway gained much of its fame through the advertising efforts of automobile manufacturers.

State Route 4 ran from New York City northwesterly through Middletown and Monticello, Liberty and Roscoe, then on to Buffalo. This was the route used by the White Motorcar Company to transport its vehicles from its assembly plant in Cleveland to its home office in New York City in the early 1900s. According to Manville B. Wakefield in *To the Mountains by Rail*, the president of the White Motorcar Company named the route the Liberty Highway because the Sullivan County village was one of the more prominent stops along the way.

In an effort to publicize its vehicles, White commissioned a film crew to travel along the Liberty Highway, shooting several thousand feet of film, much of it in and around Liberty. In fact, Wakefield relates that a great hoopla surrounded the release of this footage, and it was shown with enthusiasm throughout the county.

Before long, other automobile manufacturers began capitalizing on the notoriety of this section of road. Maxwell Motor Cars were built in Buffalo, and the company was headquartered in New York City, so they too began traveling the Liberty Highway. Buicks and Hudsons were also routed that way. By the 1920s, the Liberty Highway had become so well known that newspapers were running stories and photographs of it, and of the county in general. It was soon common for automobile manufacturers to use Sullivan County resorts and places of interest in their advertising.

But Liberty Highway promotions aside, Route 4 was not much of a highway, even by 1920 standards. As Sullivan County's reputation as a resort haven spread, traffic on the two-lane road increased. Wakefield cites a twelve-hour traffic count along the route in 1932 (it was redesignated Route 17 in 1930) of more than 88,000 cars. This provided impetus to call for a new highway system, and the present four-lane Quickway.

Many of us have memories, fond or otherwise, of old Route 17—the steep grade just south of Wurtsboro which made a sharp turn under the railroad bridge, the Bridgeville bridge, the bumper-to-bumper traffic every summer weekend. Perhaps the next time you catch a glimpse of that BMW gliding through the perilous curves of the Hawk's Nest you'll allow your imagination to wander a bit, and the car will become a White and the road will become the Liberty Highway. For although we've come a long way in the seventy years since the first ad, we really haven't traveled very far at all.

Sullivan Was Slow to Enter the Fast Lane

IN THE EARLY 1900s, vacationers traveling to the burgeoning resort area of Sullivan County had little choice in terms of transportation. The railroads thrived on vacationing travelers and catered to them to the point of publishing guides to the resorts, or "summer homes."

In the 1920s, with the increase in availability and popularity of the automobile, however, things began to change. The car provided an alternative to train travel, and many vacationers began driving Route 4 into Sullivan County. With the increasing traffic, however, this two-lane road soon became overcrowded and dangerous; a third lane was added in the early '30s, but there was still too much traffic for the highway to handle, and it got worse every year.

This led to a cry for the new highway system, one that could handle the traffic to the resort areas of Sullivan County, as well as link New York City with Binghamton. Thus was the Quickway born.

It seemed to take forever to build the new road, and the project went far from smoothly. I lived in Rock Hill in those days, right on Old Route 17, and vividly recall waiting for what seemed like hours in our driveway for an opening in the bumper-to-bumper traffic that would allow me to get to Monticello. For that reason, I suppose most residents favored building the new highway, but they almost certainly did not expect the inconvenience the construction caused.

PLACES OF INTEREST

The considerable blasting required to cut through the rock in the way of the new road was not done without incident. A stray rock shot into the air by one blast shattered the rear window on my family's new Chevrolet as it stood in our driveway. Vibrations from the blasts made dishes fall from kitchen shelves and plaster drop from ceilings in many homes. We were eating lunch one afternoon when a particularly strong blast shook the house enough to break several dishes in the kitchen cupboard. Another blast cracked the foundation of our house. Our neighbors suffered similar fates.

Many families were displaced by the construction, their homes moved to make room for the highway. Properties were divided by the great expanse; neighbors were separated. "We were newlyweds living with my in-laws in the old family house on south Main Street in Liberty," Pat Slaver recalls. "They told us they had to tear the house down to make room for the new road. This was a magnificent old stone house with a lot of sentimental attachment. My father-in-law had built it himself, and all his kids were born in the house. We were all quite upset about losing it. They began demolishing it, then decided their plans had changed—they didn't need to tear it down after all. But it was too late."

A second Slaver house, located nearby, was moved to avoid demolition. "We watched the movers take it up the hill," Pat says. "They managed to accomplish it without cracking a wall."

Among the other Liberty landmarks displaced by the construction were Sam Siegel's store and house, the Berson's, the Behren's, and Etess' Poultry Plant.

Former Sullivan County Treasurer Donald Baker has less painful memories of the construction project. His son, Donald Jr., was asked to cut the ribbon to open the portion of the road from Monticello to Parksville. "Harry Borden was chairman of the board of supervisors then," he says. "He asked me if I would allow Donnie [to cut the ribbon], so his mother, Agnes slipped him a pair of round-edge scissors to do the job."

Governor Averill Harriman was on hand for the gala celebration opening the road, and was accompanied by his dog, Brun. Major resort owners, who had lobbied vigorously for the new road, were also present, basking in the light of what for them was a major coup.

It is possible, however, that the building of the Quickway came too late to save the resorts. The automobile and the airplane had made traveling to far away places too easy, too commonplace. The days when the railroad delivered passengers where they wanted them to go, not necessarily where the travelers wanted to go, of leisurely train rides with plenty of reading material touting the benefits of the Sullivan County resorts, were no more. Hotel men had no such control over the family vacationing in the automobile, and Route 17 or no, the resort industry was never the same.

A Cop on a Harley

ONE OF MY EARLIEST RECOLLECTIONS of Old Route 17 is that of the dashing New York State Trooper who used to park his motorcycle next to our house in Rock Hill to watch for speeders.

Our house was on the corner of Old Route 17 and the road that served as the entrance to the Rock Hill Drive-In Theatre. Many mornings during warm weather, Trooper Peter Gromacki would sit and wait on that drive-in road, secluded from the view of passing motorists by our house. I was usually close by, at first watching from a safe distance, admiring the bike and the uniform, later actually talking with him, all the while secretly wanting to take the bike for a ride. There are few things more impressive to a four-year-old boy than a man in uniform and a flashy bike.

For a few summers, at least, a morning chat with Pete Gromacki was part of my life. Perhaps that is one reason that to this day it is impossible for me to think of Old Route 17 without thinking of Trooper Gromacki and his Harley-Davidson. Perhaps that's why I felt compelled after all these years to track him down. For me, no mention of the old road would be complete without Pete.

From 1952 to 1957, Trooper Pete Gromacki was the lone motorcycle cop assigned to the Wurtsboro barracks, and one of only four in all of Troop C, which then served Sullivan County. "There were only about thirty of us statewide at the time," he told me. "Years before that, before the days of sustained high speed traffic, there were

PLACES OF INTEREST

many more, maybe a hundred or a hundred and fifty, but by the early '50s the number had dwindled."

It wasn't long before state troopers on motorcycles would vanish completely. New highways such as the Quickway helped see to that. Suddenly, the trooper on motorcycle was as out of place as he would have been on horseback. "Things were so different when I started on the bike in '52," Gromacki said. "In fact, I didn't even have a radio on the bike in the early days. If the barracks wanted to get hold of me, they had to call Vapnek's garage in Monticello or some other spot along the way and leave a message. They'd hang a towel out so I'd see it and stop in."

The trooper's main job in those days was traffic control, and it wasn't easy. There were simply too many cars for Old Route 17 to handle, and too few patrolmen. "We had only one car and one motorcycle in Wurtsboro until 1954," Gromacki recalled. "Then we went to two cars and a cycle, and eventually to five men. We used to work twenty-four hours a day back then, and slept at the barracks. The traffic was always a nightmare. We'd have cars backed up from Wurtsboro to Rock Hill on most weekends, and if you have an accident or anything on top of that, it was even worse."

In fact, it was the overcrowding of the two-lane highway that ultimately led to the construction of the Quickway. A serious accident, in which a runaway truck plowed into an oncoming lane of traffic, helped fuel the push for the new road. "It wasn't at all unusual to have bumper-to-bumper traffic for miles and miles," Gromacki remembers. "We used to use traffic cones to create three lanes out of two. We'd have two lanes going toward Monticello on Friday and Saturday, and two lanes going back toward the city on Sunday."

The problems with traffic abounded under ideal conditions. Add a little inclement weather, and things really got out of hand. "To make matters worse, department regulations wouldn't allow us to take the bike out in the rain," he said. "So we had just the car."

The new, four-lane Route 17 was completed by the late 1950s, and the need for a motorcycle policeman lessened. By 1957, Pete Gromacki was off his bike for good. He advanced rapidly through the trooper ranks, however, and I kept track of his progress, most often with the help of my mother's sharp eyes. "I see where Pete

Gromacki made corporal," she'd say. "Remember when he used to sit out by the house on his motorcycle?"

Gromacki became commander of Troop F in 1977 and retired as major in 1984. Today, he works as a private investigator in Orange County. Through it all, he says, he's never forgotten his days as a motorcycle cop on Old Route 17.

"Sure, I remember those days," he said. "I could never forget the bike. I still have a trail bike which my son and I ride in the woods from time to time. And you know what? I'd go back to being a trooper on a bike tomorrow." Perhaps then he could give me the ride on the flashy Harley-Davidson the four-year-old in the house in Rock Hill never got.

Chapter Three

Recreation

The Art of Chewing's Blackest Era

THERE is a major advertising campaign underway—perhaps you've seen or heard the commercials—heralding the return of a black licorice gum that was popular among youngsters of another era. This gum has been re-issued from time to time to enthusiastic response from those who remember the taste from their childhood.

A sixty-something-year-old man I know excitedly announced that he had rediscovered the gum, and offered me a piece, which I declined. "You might as well chew blacktop from the road," I said.

"I used to do that, too," he assured me.

I assumed he was pulling my leg, and did not respond, but he continued. "I'm serious," he said. "A lot of us kids used to chew tar in the '40s. We'd go by the road after it had been redone and pick the tar off the side of the road and chew it. It would get softer and softer the more you chewed on it. It was great. It tasted good, stayed together in your mouth, and wouldn't crumble."

I was taken totally by surprise. Why would anyone chew tar from the road? I decided to check into it further, and I believe I may have discovered an activity which, if not exclusive to Sullivan County, was certainly exclusive to rural America.

My first instinct was to ask Yits Kantrowitz about it. Yits is in his mid-fifties, and works in the town of Fallsburg highway department as a purchasing agent. If Sullivan County kids really chewed tar in the '40s, he'd know about it, I reasoned, and he'd also be able to tell me what was in the stuff that might make anyone want to chew on it.

He said he'd never heard of such a thing. "Gum was readily available," he said. "Why would anyone chew on tar?"

RETROSPECT

"My sentiments, exactly," I said. "What's in the stuff anyway? Isn't it like pebbles and oil?"

"No, there are no stones in it. It is a petroleum-based asphalt product, though. I can't imagine chewing it," he said.

But to my surprise, several other people of the same age group confirmed that tar-chewing was, indeed, a popular pastime in the '40s. "We always called it pitch," one person told me. "We chewed it because our parents did, I guess. We'd find a job where they were using it, and get a chunk, and tear off strips. It'd be hard at first, but after you sucked on it for a while, it would get a certain consistency. I don't think it had the same chemical base the stuff they use today does."

"And lots of kids did it?" I asked.

"It was standard procedure," he said. "At least for boys. I never saw a girl chew pitch."

But I found one who did. "I used to chew it," one fifty-something-year-old woman told me. "It tasted great. Your saliva would soften it as you chewed. I don't know if I'd do it today, though. I think the tar they use on the roads now is different somehow."

"We used to find a patch of road where they had just finished tarring, and get a chunk," another man in his late fifties told me. "Or sometimes you could find a lot of it around a pole, where it had been bunched up and hadn't hardened."

I have now spoken with a number of people, both men and women, in that same age group. Some of them had never heard of anyone chewing tar, nor could they imagine anyone wanting to. Several others, however, assured me that it was a common practice. No one could tell me why, however, though Bert Haimann of Mountaindale offered one explanation. "I always heard that it actually cleaned your teeth," he said. "The abrasive nature of it, combined with some chemical in it was supposed to be very good for your teeth."

Fred Albrecht of White Lake told me that he and his friends chewed tar from around the railroad tracks in Monticello in the early '30s. "We'd generally whack off a hunk of tar and chew it," he wrote. "There really wasn't much taste to it, but I guess it made our teeth white."

RECREATION

Robert Karasik of Monticello also chewed tar in the early '30s. "When we were kids, we always chewed tar. We didn't have the money for gum, and the tar was supposed to be good for the teeth."

John Bowers chewed tar in Divine Corners in the early to mid-1940s. "This was something that would take place on extra-warm days in the spring, when the tar would bubble up on the roadway and become soft. We would dig up a glob about the size of a marble, put it in our mouth and chew. I thought it had a pretty good taste, and it didn't cost anything. It was a good substitute for gum, which was hard to get way out in the country where we lived."

I discovered that the practice of chewing tar was not confined to Sullivan County, nor even to rural America. Dorothy Benton of Livingston Manor chewed tar in Elmira in the late 1920s and early '30s. "We would eagerly await evening, when the streets were being tarred. As soon as the workmen left and the tar carts cooled off, we would scoop up a tablespoon full and start chewing. We moved from Elmira to Firthcliffe, New York, and lo and behold, it was being done there. My husband was born and raised in White Sulphur Springs, and tells me they also waited for the tar men to leave and would dip into the tar barrels and chew it. Perhaps it was a coincidence that most of the kids who chewed it had pearly white and stronger teeth," she said.

Bob Mierop of Grahamsville lived in Kingston when he began chewing tar in the late 1930s. "Along the West Shore Railroad tracks, there was a tar plant that us kids used to get chewing tar from. There was a half barrel there that caught the overflow from the valves when they filled the trucks. There was usually some water in the barrel, and that made the tar easy to handle prior to chewing. We'd chew until our teeth, chins, and hands were covered. We'd then cross the tracks to the cider mill and bum sweet cider to remove the tar before we went home."

Joseph Devlin of Summitville chewed tar in the Woodside area of Queens in the early '30s. "The main reason was to save our pennies for Saturday matinees—serials and cowboys."

Marie Fahrenholz of Callicoon chewed tar in the '30s and '40s in Philadelphia, and so did all of her friends.

Reverend J. David Stanway, an Episcopal priest in Monticello, grew up in Montreal, Canada, and chewed tar in the late '40s and early '50s. "There were two sources I remember. One was road crews who melted the stuff in a gas-heated portable unit and poured it into cracks in the road. The other was a similar unit used by roofers on the flat roofs of townhouses. The choice pieces were on the heating unit itself—no dirt!"

Harold Shaw of Kauneonga Lake admitted he had never chewed tar, but pointed out that the practice was discussed in detail in the book, *You Must Remember This*, an oral history of Manhattan from the 1890s to World War II.

Finally, although Dorothy Benton suggested I try finding some road tar and chewing it myself, John Bowers warned against it. "The tar we chewed back then was a coal tar product," he wrote. "The products used today are a petroleum product, and I don't believe anyone could chew this and not have ill effects."

Fishing With Your Bare Hands?

MY BEST FRIEND BOB always knew more about fishing than any other kid in the neighborhood. When the weather was nice, Bob and I would usually set aside a couple of days for taking our fishing rods down to the far side of the lower of Davies Lakes in Rock Hill and spend the mornings reeling in fish. Lots of fish. We always prided ourselves on our selection of fishing spots and on the fact that we could catch more fish than anyone else.

On one such occasion, we took our friend Mike along. Mike had just moved to the area from Long Island, and Bob and I had promised to show him how to fish. He didn't have a fishing rod, but he brought along a beer can, fishing line, some bacon and a hook.

"Whatcha gonna do with that stuff?" Bob wanted to know.

"Fish with it," Mike told him. "This is all anyone uses to fish with where I come from."

Neither Bob nor I had ever seen anything like it, and we told him so. But Mike wrapped the fishing line around the beer can, fastened the hook to it, attached the bacon as bait and threw the line into the water. Holding the beer can longways in both hands, he proceeded to feed out line and reel it back in by revolving the can. We couldn't believe it, but Mike caught as many fish as we did.

RECREATION

I have always been quite impressed with the fishing display Mike put on that morning, and to this day, whenever anyone begins talking about fancy fishing equipment, I can't help but think of Mike's beer can.

When I told him about it, Bert Haimann of Mountaindale was singularly unimpressed. "We used to catch fish without any equipment at all," he informed me. "No rod, no line, no hook, no bait."

"Okay, I'll bite," I told him. "How'd you do it?"

"We'd wade into the middle of a stream, wait until the water cleared up a bit, then reach down into the water until we found a big rock. We'd run our hands around the rock until we found a crevice, reach in, and scoop out the fish. Then we'd move on to another rock and do the same thing."

"There would be fish inside the rock?" I asked.

"Always," he said. "I'm not sure why, but that's invariably where the fish would be. All the guys used to fish that way."

"You'd just reach into the cracks in the rocks and come out with fish?" I said.

"That's right. And after a while, each guy would have his own favorite rocks that he'd work regularly. Of course, sometimes you'd reach under and come out with a giant water snake. That would usually scare you off the idea for a couple of days."

"Where'd you used to fish like that," I asked. "In the Neversink River?"

"No, the river was always too deep for that kind of fishing," he said. "We used to fish all the small streams around Mountaindale, though."

At first I wasn't sure whether or not to believe Bert's story. I thought that perhaps kids had tried to catch fish with their hands—we've probably all tried that—but to actually catch them that way on a regular basis? Could it be that his memories were just a bit embellished?

Then I remembered that Bert was one of the first people to tell me about chewing road tar. I hadn't believed that at first, either. So, I decided, maybe kids did used to catch fish with their bare hands. Maybe Bert wasn't exaggerating.

As I soon learned, catching fish with bare hands was apparently once a popular pastime in Sullivan County and elsewhere. A gentleman from Grahamsville called to say that you couldn't catch real fish with your bare hands, only crayfish. "It must have been crayfish they were catching," he insisted. But others disagreed.

Lou Fox, a former deputy supervisor in the town of Liberty, told me that fishing without the benefit of rod or reel was a common activity when he was a boy, some sixty-five years ago. "My friend, Ken Fisk, was particularly good at this technique," he said. "We'd wade into a stream, locate a good spot, and feel around for fish. I think it was quite a popular activity back then."

Fox's friend, Ken Fisk, confirmed this in a letter. "We used to catch fish with our hands while we were young, always trout," he wrote. "This is what they used to call 'fingering trout.' Find an overhanging bank along the stream where the flow of water went under it, reach your hand in, find a nice trout, run your hand under their belly and get your fingers in their gills and then pull them out. It was against the law to do this, but I guess we were lucky; we never got caught."

This disregard for the law notwithstanding, Ken Fisk went on to become a town of Liberty justice.

Donald MacInnes of Lew Beach also caught trout with his bare hands, and not just in Sullivan County. "As a boy in the north of Scotland, before coming to America, my friends and I would catch trout by hand," he writes. "It was called 'tickling.' Later, as a young man married to a lady whose folks had a summer house in Lew Beach, her brother and I would do this in the Mary Smith Brook. Tickling and taking (not too many) of our clean, cold fresh water little friends in this way is something an aging warrior will always remember."

Morris Gold, who grew up in South Fallsburg in the 1960s, wrote to say that kids in his neighborhood fished not only with their hands, but with other odd items as well. "A yearly event that got all the kids on Maple Street and Lakeland Drive crazy with anticipation was the annual running of the 'suckers,'" he wrote. "These fish, usually weighing from two to four pounds, would spawn in a brook that led into Pleasure Lake. Each spring, the call 'the suckers are running' would bring us all running to the stream. While wading in water up to our knees, we would pull these fish out, utilizing several methods, including, but not limited to, baseball bats, fishing nets, dropping rocks on them, and yes, even our bare hands."

Mike Jahrling of Wurtsboro fished for trout with his brother, Ed. Both used nothing but their hands. "We hardly ever walked in the water, though," he noted. "We would find a nice deep hole with a large rock or undercut in it. If we did it slowly enough, we could slip our hand in and feel for the fish, find their belly and tickle it slowly. This is the God's honest truth, the fish seemed to fall asleep and then we would grab them."

And just in case I still had trouble believing that fish could be caught with the bare hands, Mike had a suggestion. "Give me a call someday. We can set a date, and I'll catch one for you," he offered.

Home of Spalding Bats

FOR MORE THAN 100 YEARS, baseball and the name Spalding, as in sporting goods, have gone hand-in-hand. For a portion of that time, Sullivan County figured prominently in the association.

The sporting goods company grew out of a small business started by professional baseball player Albert Goodwill Spalding in 1876. Spalding manufactures a full line of athletic equipment, including baseballs, (they made the official major league baseball every year from 1876 to 1976) baseball gloves, and, for a time, baseball bats. It was the baseball bat which linked the firm to Sullivan County.

John Fanton Sherwood owned and operated a baseball bat factory in Livingston Manor which, from 1877 to 1900, claimed to have made every baseball bat sold under the Spalding name. Sherwood started his factory in 1868 on the raceway in back of the island where the present Livingston Manor School is located. He began his operation with just one used wood turner, and initially made just maple table legs.

Before long, he had built his mill into a thriving enterprise employing twenty-two hand turners, and he had expanded his line to include Indian clubs, dumbbells and baseball bats, according to the *Pioneer*, a history of the area compiled by Joseph Willis.

Maple was alright for the table legs, Indian clubs and dumbbells—but for baseball bats, Sherwood needed ash. Northern white ash is the only wood suitable for the construction of a bat. Ash is a strong, hard wood with a high resistance to shock and a great deal of elasticity. To make bats, ash logs were first debarked and cut into forty-inch-long sections, called bolts. These bolts, in turn, were split into wedge-shaped sections called splits, which were turned by hand in the Sherwood plant and eventually formed into rough bats. These were shipped to Spalding for finishing and branding with the company logo.

Somewhere around the turn of the century, Sherwood began to manufacture bowling pins as well. By 1905, when he moved his factory to a roomier location, bowling pins had become his main product. Although that factory was destroyed by fire in 1916, it was rebuilt, and the Sherwoods continued to manufacture bowling pins. The firm eventually bought a 5,000-acre farm on which they grew the lumber to be used in the mill. At its peak, the mill turned out more than two thousand bowling pins a day. These were sold directly to bowling alleys at first, but were later marketed to equipment supply companies such as Brunswick, one of the best known names in bowling equipment.

Still, the baseball bats have provoked the most interest. Some Sullivan County residents told me there were other baseball bat factories in the county at one time or another. Some said that the factory in Livingston Manor continued to manufacture bats until the 1950s; others claimed that bats were never made there—baseball bats came only from Parksville, they said.

There seems little doubt that the Sherwood plant once manufactured the Spalding bats, since this has been well documented, including a detailed treatment in the *Pioneer*, a publication that was put together in 1939 for the dedication of the Livingston Manor School. But when did the manufacture of these bats cease? And were there other baseball bat factories in the county?

Spalding couldn't clear up the controversy. Shirley Brisbois, the company's manager of consumer relations, told me there is no easy way to know for sure whether Spalding ever bought bats from the Sherwood mill, or if so, in what years. "I doubt if we'd have any record of where the rough bats came from at all, since we didn't actually own the mills," she said. "Of course, it's entirely possible that we bought bats from both Livingston Manor and Parksville, but I wouldn't know where to begin to look to find out for sure."

RECREATION

Bill Sarles of Livingston Manor proved helpful, however. "I worked for Burr Sherwood in his bowling pin factory for twenty-four years, until they shut down," he wrote me. "Sherwood's made all the Spalding baseball bats right here in Livingston Manor. I am well acquainted with the factory. All the turners who made the bats lived right here in Livingston Manor. Some of the squares used to make the baseball bats could have been bought in Parksville or other towns. I have a letterhead, 'J. F. Sherwood—Manufacturer baseball bats, paper rollers, etc., etc.' from Jan. 4th, 1884."

This bit of information piqued my curiosity enough. I thought Sarles might have other remnants which might prove noteworthy—a picture of the factory, for instance. It took me over a week to reach him by telephone. He said in his letter that he spent a lot of time in his garden and wasn't near the phone very often. "Keep trying," he had advised.

When I finally spoke to him, I was, at first, disappointed. My questions about pictures, especially those which might prove that bats were made at that plant, drew a negative response. "I don't believe I ever had a picture of the factory," he told me. "Hard to believe, because I collect lots of old stuff like that, especially pictures and post cards. I've got loads of them, but I don't think I've got any pictures of the factory at all, or even of the raceway in back of the island where it was first located. Nothing from that part of town."

I explained the disagreements surrounding the stories of the bat factory, and how some people claim there never were baseball bats made in Livingston Manor. "Oh, I'm sure they made bats here, all right," he said. "I don't think they made them anywhere else in the county, either. In fact, I have an invitation to the Spalding baseball dance at the Island Park Casino. This was a dance they held every year for the bat turners and their families. I also have a picture of the Spalding baseball team which represented the factory. William White, a former motor vehicles commissioner, and John White, who played on the New York Giants for John McGraw, were both on the team. I think he was the only player from Sullivan County to ever make the big leagues."

"Now I'm really interested," I said. "Would it be possible for me to stop by some time and look at these things?"

RETROSPECT

"Don't mind you coming by at all," he said. "But you're going to have to give me a chance to dig them up. I've got an awful lot of stuff to go through, and right now I spend all my time working in my garden. I've got to get my garden in, but once I get through with that, I'll give you a call, and you're welcome to see whatever I got."

Shortly after meeting me at the door of his River Street home, Sarles said, "I know more about Livingston Manor history than anybody alive." And he wasn't kidding.

He was seventy-eight years old, but he didn't look a day over sixty. Working had kept him young, he said. "I worked for the Sherwood's at their latter-day plant for twenty-four years, until the day they shut down," he told me. "But that's not why I know what I do. I'm very interested in the history of this area, and I collect postcards and pictures and letterheads and things."

"You said on the phone that you had pictures of the Spalding baseball team," I reminded him.

"That's right," he nodded, "Now, remember, the Spaldings were the town team. Since the plant was closely aligned with Spalding, and was such an important fixture in the town, they named themselves after Spalding."

"One of them was the only guy from Sullivan County to play in the major leagues?" I asked.

"John White," Bill said. "Played center field for the New York Giants under John McGraw."

"Well, I checked, but I couldn't find any record of a John White ever playing with the Giants," I said.

"I'm sure he did," he insisted. "Talk around town was that McGraw called him the laziest baseball player he ever saw. Turned to him on the bench one day, and he was sleeping there."

"Okay," I said. "I'll do some more checking. What about the baseball bat factory?"

"You wanted proof that bats were made here in Livingston Manor, right?" he asked. With that, he produced four large photo albums, opened one, and began to slowly turn the plastic pocket pages. "I've got a lot of great stuff in here," Bill said as he paused at various hand-written bills of sale from different establishments—dry goods stores, grist mills, liveries, acid factories. All the bills were from the 1800s or so.

RECREATION

"Now here's one from the J. F. Sherwood factory," he said, pointing to a faded letterhead on blue-lined paper. The letterhead read, "J. F. Sherwood, Manufacturer of Hardwood and Hemlock Lumber; All Kinds Turned Stuff; Ball Bats, Paper Rollers, Etc.; Livingston Manor, N.Y." It was dated Jan. 4, 1884, and bore the signature of J. F. Sherwood.

"That's John Fanton Sherwood," Bill said. "But here's one I find even more interesting." He pointed to a similar letterhead, this one dated May 25, 1887. It read, "J. D. Sherwood, Established 1873; Manufacturer of Ball Bats, and Indian Clubs, Dumb Bells, Paper Rollers, and Rock Maple for Export; All Kinds of Turned Stuff."

"Don't know of any J. D. Sherwood," Bill said. "Could be a printing mistake, I don't know." Except the note on which the letterhead appeared was signed J. D. Sherwood.

Nevertheless, there it was, in faded black and yellowed white—baseball bats were once made in Livingston Manor.

But I still didn't know when they stopped making them, and I wanted a bat. "You really should talk to Clarence Sherwood," Bill said. "He's John Fanton Sherwood's grandson, and he lives right here in town. He's probably got more information on the factory, and maybe even a bat."

"I have a feeling I'll be seeing you again," I told him. "You've got some great stuff here."

"I told you I know more about Livingston Manor than anyone," Bill said as he walked me to the door.

Clarence Sherwood sounded excited when I contacted him regarding my quest for a baseball bat from the factory founded by his grandfather. He told me he had worked in the plant himself for thirty-three years, eventually serving as vice president. He had originally said he had a number of items—bowling pins, duck pins, candle pins, Indian clubs, dumbbells—from the heyday of the factory, which shut down in 1962, but no baseball bat. Now he was telling me that he had located a bat.

It wasn't actually a bat manufactured in the old factory, which was located on Sherwood's Island, he said, but one his father, Pete Sherwood, had hand-turned in the new plant, probably in the 1920s. He had asked around, he said, and a friend had come up with it from his attic.

Clarence told me that John Fanton Sherwood was indeed the sole vendor of baseball bats to the Spalding sporting goods company in the late 1800s and early 1900s. He said he had pictures of the original plant, which was moved about 1905, and of the raceway that powered it.

In the dining room of his home on Musman's Flats, my wife Debbie and I looked at the wood products spread out on the table before me. We had arrived a few minutes early, and Clarence had yet to return from town. His wife had invited us in to wait. A baseball bat, long and fat and heavy-looking, immediately captured my attention. I picked it up and looked it over.

"How old is that, would you say?" Debbie asked.

"He told me on the phone that it was from the '20s," I said. "But from what I know about bat design, I'd say this is more of a late '30s or early '40s bat." Clarence walked in at just that moment. "That's the one," he said. "I believe that bat was hand-turned by my father in the early 1920s."

I moved over to the window to examine the bat in the sunlight. A familiar marking, vague and obscured with age, caught my eye. It was a small arc—what had once been part of an oval. Underneath, I could barely discern the letters "GG."

"I don't think this is one of your father's bats." I said. "It looks to me like it's an old Louisville Slugger." Clarence was crestfallen. I showed him the oval and the letters I had found. He couldn't see them, nor could Debbie, though she admitted there was something there. "No doubt in my mind," I said. "I'm sorry to be the one to tell you that."

"No, it's all right," he said dejectedly. "I'm sure my friend actually believed it was my father's work. Makes sense, though, that it would be a Louisville Slugger."

"Why's that?" I wondered.

"Because we had thousands of them through our plant," he said. "We dried all their bats for many years."

The ash splits from which baseball bats are turned must be dried; to my knowledge, bats were always air dried, a process that normally took well over a year. "We were one of the few places around with sophisticated enough kilns to dry bats. Prior to that, bats had to be air dried, because the temperature of the kilns couldn't be controlled precisely enough," Sherwood said.

"So they never actually made bats while you worked at the factory?" I asked.

"Just the few that we'd hand-turn for special orders now and then," he said. "By the time I started there, we were so busy making bowling pins for Brunswick that we couldn't make any bats. We turned out over twenty-three hundred pins a day, you know. Bowling pins were my life for a long time."

"You sound as if you miss it," I said.

"Darn right I do," he assured me.

I picked up one of the pins from his table. "Well, they aren't baseball bats, but tell me about them anyway," I said.

Clarence Sherwood put the Louisville Slugger aside and sat down. For the moment, at least, we had both forgotten our disappointment.

The Hemlocks

THERE IS A LARGE FIELD a block off Broadway in the village of Monticello that on most spring weekend afternoons is filled with throngs of townspeople cheering for the local baseball team. Many of the spectators are shopkeepers who've closed their businesses to attend, others are village dignitaries—virtually everybody who is anybody is there.

It's 1876, and this isn't just *any* baseball team—it's the Hemlocks, and they rule the world of semi-pro baseball.

For five years or so, beginning in the late 1870s, the Hemlocks were the most renowned baseball team east of the Cincinnati Red Stockings. Squads came from far and wide to challenge the Hemlocks' superiority, and, more

Hemlocks' jersey. Monticello's baseball team ruled the world of semi-pro ball in the late 19th century. (Sullivan County Historical Society)

RETROSPECT

often than not, left duly impressed. From Middletown and Honesdale, from Brooklyn and Jersey City, the challengers arrived, only to find the Hemlocks as formidable as their reputation.

Major league baseball had yet to establish itself; the National Baseball League had just begun play. Salaries for major leaguers weren't substantial, and many of the most talented players were found in the semi-pro ranks. Almost every town had a team, and the better teams sooner or later found their way to Monticello to test themselves against the best.

George Ludington. Lud was the heart and soul of the Hemlocks during their heyday. (Sullivan County Historical Soci-

The Hemlocks played their home games at Bennett Field, which was just off Broadway on Mill Street (now St. John Street). The field was outlined by a picket fence on one end and a stone wall on the other. It would be the site upon which the Monticello High School would later be constructed, but from 1876 to 1881 the Hemlocks called its cozy confines home.

George Ludington was the captain and manager of the team. He was a Monticello native, and a popular young man known as much for his inspiration as for his baseball ability, which was considerable. Besides Ludington, who most often played catcher, the original team members included pitcher Bill Hindley, first baseman Frank Holley, second baseman Oscar Olmstead, third baseman Frank Snook, shortstop Thomas Watts, and outfielders Charles and Henry LeBarbier and Joseph Merritt.

Although these ballplayers made up a stalwart contingent, it wasn't until the following year, when pitcher Blake Mapledoram arrived, that the Hemlocks' legend really began. Mapledoram was an incredibly strong man, made so by years of hard labor on his family's farm. He featured a blistering fastball and a wicked curve, and the Hemlocks seldom found themselves falling behind their opponents when he was on the mound. Still, it wasn't without a struggle that he found himself in a Hemlocks uniform.

Despite his abilities, he watched from the sidelines in 1876, unable to crack the lineup. Only after a group of prominent villagers, a Mapledoram fan club, so to speak, formed their own team with Blake

RECREATION

as its hurler did Mapledoram get his chance to pitch. He totally mastered the powerful Hemlock bats, striking out player after player and defeating the Hemlocks in a series of exhibitions. From that point on, he was the Hemlock hurler.

Mapledoram was so good that he eventually moved on to play professional ball. An arm injury ended his career before he made it to the National League or the American Association of Baseball Clubs, at that time baseball's major leagues. Following that career-ending injury, he umpired for several years in the professional ranks before retiring from the game to enter the engineering profession.

Blake Mapledoram. The Hemlocks rose to power when Mapledoram and his blazing fastball were added to the roster. (Sullivan County Historical Society)

While Mapledoram was a Hemlock, the team was simply awesome, and over the next few years Ludington added players as needed to stay one step ahead of the competition. Although the majority of the team was from Monticello, Lud always had just enough out-of-town firepower on hand to win, regardless of the opposition. At one point, there were three professionals playing fairly regularly on the Hemlocks, including Powell and Lewis from Tarrytown, and a player named Mitchell from New York City. Of the three, Mitchell is by far the most interesting.

Mitchell, it turns out, was not the ballplayer's real name at all. In his book *Old Monticello*, Edward F. Curley identified him as a former major league player named Reipschoqw, who had been blacklisted from the American Association for gambling. Although he called Mitchell "a marvelous player," Curley alludes to a game the Hemlocks played against Honesdale which many felt Mitchell, catching for Monticello, was paid to lose.

Curley further notes that Reipschoqw was later inexplicably reinstated by the American Association and went on to catch for the New York Mutuals, league champions in "1883 or 1884."

The *Baseball Encyclopedia* includes no one named Reipschoqw, but does list Charley Reipschlager, who was indeed the back-up catcher on the New York Metropolitans when they won the American Association championship. Reipschlager was born in New York

City around 1855, and began playing baseball in 1872, catching for the Silver Stars, New York's amateur champions. From there he made the rounds, and his path to the mountains was a circuitous one.

According to an 1883 edition of the *New York Clipper*, he played for teams from Orange and Jersey City, New Jersey; Auburn, Albany and Brooklyn, New York; and Worcester and New Bedford, Massachusetts, before joining the Metropolitans. The *Clipper* article makes no mention of a tenure with the Hemlocks, though there seems little doubt that it was Reipschlager who played in Monticello as Mitchell.

Reipschlager had a reputation as a rough-and-tumble player, and a carouser. A letter, written to the editor of *The Sporting Life* in 1887 by the manager of the Cleveland team, defended Reipschlager, who had been accused of drinking heavily to the detriment of his teammates. "There are a lot of dirty squibs going the rounds of the papers to the effect that Charley Reipschlager is not and cannot keep from drinking and will not long be able to keep his position with the Cleveland club," the letter began. "I wish to say that 'Reip' is not only playing excellent ball, but is behaving himself as well as any man in the team, and that his play and behavior are more than satisfactory to the management of the Cleveland club." The letter is signed by J. A. Williams, manager.

Charlie Reipschlager. This is the only known picture of the ringer who played for the Hemlocks and then on the champion New York Mets. (Author's collection)

Regardless of the truth of these rumors, there is no doubt that Reipschlager was one of the most colorful baseball players of his era, and at least part of that era he spent in Monticello, catching for the Hemlocks whenever they needed outside help to maintain their baseball dynasty.

No dynasty lasts forever, though, and the Hemlocks' was no exception. Ludington left the team following the 1880 season, and that was the beginning of the end. He had been the heart and soul of the team, and his departure left a void that could not be filled. First baseman Frank Holley and shortstop Thomas Watts left shortly thereafter, and when Blake Mapledoram went on to the professional ranks, the Hemlocks had simply lost too much of their firepower.

Gone were the days when Ludington, Holley, Watts, Frank Snook and Charles LeBarbier could choose any four townspeople and beat off the challenge of most any opponent. By 1881, not even a "ringer" like Charley Reipschlager could have saved them.

Memories of Monticello Amusement Park

MY FATHER, when properly moved, was a truly great storyteller. He was particularly fond of relating tales of his youth—the experiences of a youngster growing up in Depression-era Monticello. It was, to be sure, a far different Monticello from the village in which I grew up.

It was largely through the vivid verbal portraits my father painted that I learned about the Monticello of the 1920s and '30s. Despite his considerable talents, though, it wasn't until I came across some old photographs that I began to appreciate the magnitude of one of his favorite subjects: Monticello Amusement Park.

To fully understand, one must recall the Monticello of my youth. At that time, the west end of Broadway was intersected on the north side by Wheeler Street, subsequently a victim of urban renewal. To the northwest of Wheeler Street was a large, open field. For several years during my early youth, the circus used the field for its annual visit to the village. I can't remember much else ever happening there. I do remember that almost every time we passed by that field, my father would relate stories of the great amusement park that once occupied the site.

He admitted that his memories were vague—the park had burned when he was fairly young—but he would nonetheless describe a park that seemed so unlikely to exist in Monticello that I must have dismissed it as hyperbole. That is, until I saw the pictures. From what I've been able to ascertain, it was, for a short time, just about the most popular spot in the county.

The park was dominated by its entrance, marked by a large, tri-towered archway. It included a roller coaster, merry-go-round, fun house and various other attractions that reportedly cost its owners nearly a half million dollars— that's a half million 1920s' dollars.

One of the most popular attractions at the park was the large, domed dance hall, which provided entertainment in the form of a live band as well as shelter during inclement weather.

The park apparently enjoyed its heyday during the early 1920s. At that point, it hosted several thousand visitors each day. It seems the park closed down for a year or so in the late '20s, then reopened in 1929. With a few new attractions and some sprucing up of the existing ones, the park again began to flourish, though never approaching the popularity it once enjoyed. Of course, the Great Depression had begun, and fewer tourists were traveling to the county in general. Even so, the park did reasonably well for the next few years.

On August 16, 1932, the dance hall at the park caught fire, and it, along with a number of other attractions, burned to the ground. At the height of the summer season, the park was closed, never to reopen again. The remaining structures, including the magnificent archway entrance, were demolished some time later, leaving, by the time of my youth, not even the ruins. There was nothing about that vacant field of the 1950s to suggest that on it once stood such an incredible entertainment complex.

But neither the fire that destroyed the park, nor the passing years could totally obliterate the spectacle of what once was.

Andy McCullough of Monticello worked on construction of the park in 1923. "The swimming pool is what I remember most," he says. "It was as big as any pool at any hotel today, and I ought to know—I helped build it by hand." He also remembers the dance hall, which served more than one purpose. "They used to have basketball games in the hall. All the towns around had their own team; Monticello had two teams, Liberty had a team, Ellenville had a team. They used to play the games at the amusement park."

Ethel Bishop of Rock Hill remembers that her husband also worked on the project. "They must have had hundreds of workers there," she says. "It was quite a job to get all those attractions built. In later years, my husband and I spent a lot time there. I remember riding the roller coaster. It wasn't a very long roller coaster, but it

RECREATION

was quite steep, It really took your breath away coming over that first drop."

Mrs. Bishop also won prizes for her dancing at the park. "The ballroom was particularly splendid," she recalls. "It had a large, domed roof and a huge, multi-faceted globe hanging down from the middle of the ceiling."

Albert Stanton of Monticello supplied many of the materials used to build the dance hall. "I worked in the hardware store, which did a lot of business when they were building the park," he says. "Later, I spent many an evening there, taking my dates dancing at the ballroom. It was very romantic—this huge, spectacular ball hanging down from the middle of the ceiling, sparkling and reflecting the light."

Patricia Gardner of Monticello has similar memories of the structure. "The dance floor was like glass," she remembers. "I spent many enjoyable evenings there as a teenager, as did many of the local girls. But my first experience at the amusement park goes back a few years before that. I grew up in Middletown, but often came to visit my aunt and uncle in Woodbourne. One summer evening they took me to the park and it was simply marvelous. I'll never forget the gateway. The half moons on either side were lit up and it was a breathtaking sight."

Sylvia Zarin of Monticello was in the third grade when the park first opened. "It was the spring of 1924, and each student received a free pass. To use it was something big and spectacular. It opened three or four consecutive springs, but each year seemed less of a success than the previous year. It tried again a few years later, but that was the last of it. To this day, every time I ride past the spot I think of it, and sometimes tell my children and grandchildren about it."

The Monticello Amusement Park was a popular attraction, but not universally so. "There were some businessmen who felt the park was pulling people away from their places," Andy McCullough says. "In fact, it was heavily rumored and commonly believed at the time that the fire which closed the park was set by a business rival jealous of its success. Of course, there was never any proof."

Whether the fire was deliberately set or not is today a moot point. Not even fire can destroy memories.

RETROSPECT

Perhaps, in some way, the field I remembered as a youth is symbolic of the changes Monticello has undergone over the years. The popular fun spot of the '20s gave way to the ruins of the '30s; the vacant field of the '50s gave way to the supermarket of the '60s, to the abandoned building of the '70s, and eventually to the revival of the '80s.

Even today, however, with most everyone agreeing the county has made its comeback, we've yet to devise the attraction to match the appeal of the wonderful, exciting, Monticello Amusement Park.

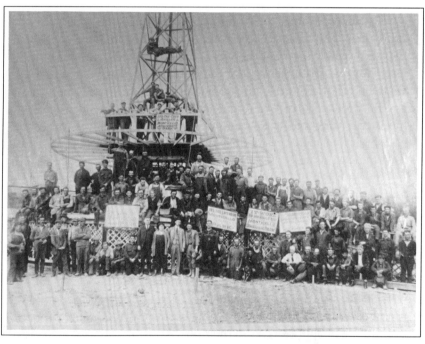

Monticello Amusement Park. Workmen pose for a photograph upon the park's completion in the 1920s. (Author's collection)

Chapter Four

Slices of Life

Barbershops: Shear Pleasure

MY BROTHER is one of those few remaining American men who prefer to get their hair cut by old-fashioned barbers in traditional barber shops. This, he tells me, is becoming an increasingly difficult task with each haircut. The barber shop, as we used to know it, is slowly vanishing from the scene, to be replaced by the "unisex hair salon."

With persistence, one can still find a barber shop, but there are far fewer than there were just a decade or so ago. Furthermore, most are manned by aging barbers, with no replacements on the horizon for when it comes time to hang up the clippers. It appears likely the day will come when the barber shop and the barber will no longer be with us.

Historians tell us that barbers have been around at least since the thirteenth century. In fact, barbers were once responsible for far more important things than cutting hair and trimming beards. Barbers in the old days doubled as dentists and surgeons, with whitening and extracting teeth and bloodletting among their most common operations. The practice of bloodletting, once believed to be the cure for virtually all ailments, is actually what led to the adoption of the red-and-white barber's pole as a symbol of the barber shop. In those days, it was common for a patient to grasp a pole with one hand in order to facilitate the flow of blood during the bloodletting. The poles were painted red to minimize the discoloration from bloodstains. When not in use, the pole was frequently wrapped in white gauze and hung outside the shop as an advertisement of the barber-surgeon's ability. Rather gruesome, indeed.

RETROSPECT

This bit of history is not something about which most children are aware; there has to be some other reason why barbers have always been so frightening to them. I vividly remember hiding from my father whenever it was time to get my hair cut. When I finally did go, the process didn't seem all that bad, and a lollipop was usually my reward. Nevertheless, I hid again next time my hair was due to be cut.

Broadway in Monticello was lined with barber shops when I was young, but we always frequented Angelo's, on the west end. The shop itself was fairly typical. There were several barber chairs, each with its own razor strop. There were mirrors along one wall and small glass cabinets in which sundries were stored. Each barber had a small black-and-chrome machine that dispensed hot shaving lather. There was a jar for the lollipops, and boards that fit across the arms of the barber chair to raise a child within easy reach. And, there was my favorite: row after row of hair tonics and dressings, each in its own distinctive bottle, each with its own distinctive label promising fantastic results.

Besides Angelo's, there were lots of other barber shops in Monticello. One I remember well—though I never got my hair cut there—was the Park Barber Shop on Broadway, near St. John Street. From the outside, it always looked well kept—venetian blinds, a large plant visible through the window, and the usual interior decorations.

There was Sal's, owned by the same barber who, while working at Angelo's, had given me my first haircut. There was the Carlton and the Strand, both near the center of town, and both still open into the 1980s. I'm sure there were others. Most were patronized by regular customers who seldom went elsewhere. Few men, it seemed, would trust anyone other than their regular barber to cut their hair.

Monticello, of course, was not the only town with barber shops. Old timers in Sullivan County talk about shops like J. M. Pierce's in Woodbourne and Mark Slater's in Grahamsville, where men like my grandfather went to get a little taken off the top. If memory serves, my grandfather would always emerge dapper and groomed, smelling of hair tonic and talcum powder.

Jim Wade was the barber in Eldred for many years, and Bill James of Monticello remembers the shop during the mid-'50s. "There are pictures in your mind about the shop you just don't forget," James says. "Blowing hair off the scissors onto the floor, the aroma of witch hazel and hair tonic, all pretty much the same, no matter which shop you went into."

In Barryville, it was Traver's; in Old Falls, Sandy's. In Wurtsboro it was Masten's; in Liberty, Ray Cali's. In Mountaindale, it was Jack Wack's. When that shop closed its doors sometime prior to 1950, Mountaindale was left to this day without a barber shop, leaving the men of the community to travel at least to Woodridge to get their hair cut—perhaps that's one reason Woodridge always supported two barber shops. Morris Fox, mayor of the village for a number of years, had one barber shop, with the added convenience of a shoeshine stand outside. After Fox sold his business, Max Melofsky took over the location. Meyer Denenberg was another of Woodridge's barbers in the 1940s. His shop became Moe's when he sold out to Moe Wolfer.

Barber shops were, for the most part, for men only. Occasionally a shop would allow a beauty salon to operate in the back, as did Angelo's in Monticello, Sandy's in Old Falls, or Fox's in Woodridge—but there was no mingling of the customers. Perhaps that's why the barber shop was often more than just a place to get a haircut or a shave. It also sometimes served as a neighborhood hangout. In South Fallsburg, many of the old-time politicians congregated at Shuster and Donenfeld's shop on Main Street. Marcu Langer's was also more than just a barber shop—it featured a poker table just past the chairs, and a pool table in back.

"One of the things I remember most about Langer's," one delightful old timer remarks, "is the pool table. I used to spend a lot of time there as a youngster and got to be a pretty good pool player. Another thing I'll never forget is the punch card. We used to get a card for a quarter and punch out a number to reveal a piece of paper. The paper, when unraveled, would tell you if you won a dollar, or five dollars, or whatever. Of course, most times you didn't win anything."

There was also Youngfrau's Barber Shop on Main Street in South Fallsburg, and all three shops on the street seemed to thrive.

I remember getting my hair cut in the late '60s at Vinnie's in Rock Hill. Vinnie's was like most other shops, and it always seemed that a few of us would get haircuts together. Or if one of us was getting a haircut, others might tag along to keep him company. We'd pass the time reading *Sports Illustrated* or *Sport*. Sometimes Vinnie would protest, because paying customers might pull up and see a crowd inside and not come in—no one made an appointment to get a haircut in those days.

Now, not only do most men make appointments, but they do so not with Vinnie or Sal or José, but with Rosemary or Marie or Wendy or Rebecca. The unisex salon might offer superior hair cutting and the added pleasure of having a woman fuss over you, but it can't match the old-fashioned barber shop in character or charm.

Pioneer Physicians: The Stuff of Legends

MY MOTHER has often told the story of when she was taken quite ill as an infant in the 1920s and a dedicated physician made the trip from Monticello to Woodbourne on horseback in the dead of winter to save her life. That physician was Dr. Ralph S. Breakey, and for those who knew the man, no more need be said. He remains a certified legend in Sullivan County medical annals. The man was a fixture for well over fifty years, and delivered not only all of the Conway children (a considerable task in itself), but my mother and father as well.

As difficult as it may be to believe for some of us, though, Dr. Breakey was not the first physician in Sullivan County. Indeed, as well known as he may have been in the Monticello area, there were contemporaries held in similar regard in other parts of the county.

One of the early Sullivan County physicians was Doctor Blake Wales, of the town of Neversink. Dr. Wales relocated to the county from Connecticut around 1799, and practiced medicine in Neversink and Liberty into the 1840s. Doctors in those days were required to attend to the sick across a wide area, and Dr. Wales regularly traveled throughout Chestnut Woods, Blue Mountain Settlement, Sumac Point, Parksville, and what was to become the village of Liberty, which at that time consisted only of two one-room log cabins.

SLICES OF LIFE

Dr. George Baker was the first physician in the town of Callicoon. He was born in the town of Thompson, worked for a time in New York City, where he learned his science, and then settled in Callicoon. Tales of his medical ingenuity are legendary, and include an incident that occurred in Woodbourne, while he was practicing medicine there. Dr. Baker reportedly performed one of the first tracheotomies in America while attending a sick patient; his innovative use of a lancet and goose quill not only saved the man's life, but became a standard practice in emergency medicine thereafter. Unfortunately, Dr. Baker was not the most stable man, or so history has recorded, and he abandoned medicine to pursue other endeavors, only to die impoverished and reclusive in a crude shelter in Callicoon.

There are other early Sullivan County physicians, including Dr. John Taylor of Mamakating, Dr. Benjamin Hardenburgh of Fallsburg, and Dr. John Gray of Rockland, of whom less is recorded.

Doctors began appearing in Sullivan County in fairly large numbers in the teens and '20s, and many of these physicians continued to practice for thirty years or more. There was Dr. Duggan in Bethel, Dr. Orr in Grahamsville, Dr. Munson in Woodbourne. There was Dr. Malisoff in Woodridge and Dr. Greenburg and Dr. Turner in South Fallsburg. There was Dr. Jacobs in Hurleyville, and three generations of Doctors Payne in Liberty.

One of the best remembered early doctors is Dr. McWilliams of Monticello. McWilliams's office was located on Bank Street, in the Masonic Building. He practiced well into his eighties, and often doubled as a dentist. Florence Sharkey of Monticello remembers McWilliams as the doctor who delivered her in the 1920s. "He must have been eighty or thereabouts at that time," she recalls. "Most births were home births in those days, and my mother always said that Dr. McWilliams advised her to avoid the flowery names that were popular at the time, names like Pansy and Violet and Rose. He suggested that she name me after his mother, Hortense Abigail. My sister intervened and I ended up Florence."

Another early Monticello physician was Dr. James Cauthers, whose daughter, Mildred Smith, still resides in Monticello. Mrs. Smith, now in her nineties, remembers her father as Dr. Breakey's mentor. "Dr. Breakey lived with us in Monticello for a time," she said. "My father helped him get to New York City to study medicine, and after the war, Dr. Breakey came back to Monticello to set up a practice here. My father's office was on Broadway, where the Van-Inwegan, Kenny and Sullivan funeral home is now. Most times, he'd treat people for nothing, since a lot of folks had no money back then."

Another old-timer was Dr. DeKay in Hurleyville. Abe Deutsch of Hurleyville remembers the doctor also doubled as the pharmacist. "I can remember going to his office, which of course was located in his home, as most doctor's offices were in those days, and he never wrote out a prescription. He always gave you the medicine right there. I think that was fairly unusual. Dr. DeKay was the only doctor in the area for a long time, then Dr. Jacobs came along some time later."

Of all of the early Sullivan County physicians, one of the most colorful and successful was Dr. John D. Watkins of Liberty, a prominent doctor-businessman-politician in the mid-1800s. Although his exploits considerably predate those of the other physicians chronicled here, his legacy is still intact. Dr. Watkins founded the Liberty Normal School in 1847, and eventually became superintendent of county schools, supervisor of Liberty, and a state senator. For all of those accomplishments, however, Dr. Watkins is perhaps more remembered for something else.

He built what is today the Keller Building on Main Street in Liberty, the seat of the town government. Since Dr. Watkins was quite short, the building was designed to accommodate him. Its diminutive dimensions remained for many years. "I can remember taking the children to the house to trick-or-treat in the 1930s," Grace Suslosky, of Liberty, said. "The door handles, window sills, and things were all close to the ground because he was so short. Legend always had it that he was so short because of the great eclipse of 1806, the year he was born."

Eclipse or not, it is believed that Dr. Watkins was considerably under four feet in height. There was nothing small about his generosity, though. In addition to founding the school, he also made substantial contributions to the construction of the Methodist-Episcopal Church of Liberty, the 143rd Regiment of the New York Volunteers, the Liberty fire department and numerous other charities. He also published several mathematics text books and was generally regarded as a most distinguished gentlemen, a fine example for the physicians who followed.

Shoemakers?

I'M NOT EXACTLY SURE what it says about our collective lifestyles these days, but I hardly ever hear anyone talk about shoemakers anymore. Think about it: People still wear shoes—most people I know own at least several pair—but it seems hardly anyone ever gets them repaired these days. They are more likely to wear the shoes out and then get rid of them.

Sure, someone will occasionally have heels replaced on a particularly favorite pair of shoes, or have a new pair of shoes stretched a bit, but I think a trip to the shoemaker is fairly rare. In keeping with the increasing trend toward a completely disposable economy, shoes have, for the most part, become disposable.

Such was not always the case. People living in the latter years of the 19th century probably owned just one pair of shoes or boots, or perhaps two pair—one for work and one for dress. And, as a rule, these shoes or boots had to last virtually forever. That meant extensive maintenance and repair.

Almost every small town had a shoemaker—if not more than one—a man who supported himself by making and repairing shoes. Such a business, while certainly not extinct, has become a rarity these days. *Child's Gazetteer*, published in 1873, listed well over a hundred boot and shoe manufacturers in Sullivan County, half a dozen of them large enough to take out display ads in the journal. That's not counting the general merchants who repaired and sold shoes as part of a broader overall business.

Liberty had four shoemakers: John Bengel, the Chulein Brothers, Frederick Schaeffer and Jacob Weber. Bengel and Weber were perhaps the largest. Bengel, whose business was located opposite the Methodist Church on Liberty Street, manufactured boots and shoes "from the best material" and "warrants a fit and guarantees satisfaction." Bengel also advertised repairing, "neatly done at reasonable prices."

Weber was also located on Liberty Street. He manufactured and sold "boots, ladies' and gents' shoes, gaiters, slippers, rubbers, etc." He advertised "repairing neatly done on short notice," and promised his boots were "unsurpassed for ease and comfort."

In addition, William Ernst and Eldon Fuller were located in Parksville, Jonah Davis and Samuel Jenkins in Liberty Falls (Ferndale), and David Hathaway in Stevensville (Swan Lake).

Callicoon Depot boasted six shoemakers: A.H. Bush, George Dech, Adam Metzger, Andrew Stadler, and Christian and Lewis Wagner. Woodbourne featured two: Michael Eidel and John Kneip. Eidel, located "near the cabinet shop," featured "men, women and children's boots and shoes." He made "boots and shoes to fit from good material," and also did repairing. Kneip claimed twenty-five years of experience in the business, and manufactured "boots and shoes to order, from the best of stock at the lowest price." He guaranteed "a good fit, always."

Monticello listed seven shoemaking enterprises, among them Andrew Winterberger, who worked out of a shop "a half mile east of the Exchange Hotel." In lieu of his qualifications as a manufacturer, Winterberger chose to advertise that he was also a dealer in "groceries, tobacco, kerosene oil, etc." David Blanchard, William Carpenter, George Powell, Seth Royce, Frank Shatzel, and Ryall & O'Neill also worked out of the county seat.

John K. Cooper was a manufacturer of and dealer in boots, shoes, gaiters and slippers in Thompsonville. Cooper dealt in "French and American kip and calf skins, sole and upper leather, and a general assortment of findings." "Work and goods guaranteed to give satisfaction and sold at the lowest cash price," he advertised. John McRoden also was a shoemaker in Thompsonville.

There were dozens of others throughout the county, good, hard-working men—men our contemporary society has somehow learned to do without—who kept the farmer and the merchant, the blacksmith and the lawyer, the wagon-maker and the surgeon, in shoes.

SLICES OF LIFE

One-Woman Schools

MADELINE CROSS of Woodbourne is truly one of the overlooked characters in Sullivan County history. In the tradition of Laura Ingalls Wilder, Mrs. Cross was a teacher—a schoolmarm if you will—in a one-room schoolhouse. In fact, in the eleven years she worked, beginning in 1921, Mrs. Cross taught in at least seven different one-room schoolhouses. Dozens of similar schools dotted Sullivan County in those days, some of which operated into the 1950s, and at least one of which, in Eldred, was still operating in 1960.

Mrs. Cross was a product of a one-room schoolhouse, having attended the school at Krum Settlement, near Parksville, before going on to the teachers' college at Cortland. She began her career in a schoolhouse in Briscoe, and over the years worked in Beach Ridge, White Sulphur Springs, Hasbrouck, Michigan (near Woodbourne), Thunder Hill, and Old Falls.

"All of the schools were similar," Mrs. Cross once told me. "The older kids sat on one side of the room, the younger kids on the other. The bathrooms were out back and the heat was provided by one wood stove. Water was supplied by a large bucket and a single dipper. Everyone shared it, and no one ever got sick from it."

The teacher's job was made somewhat easier by the fact that the students in the upper grades often worked with those in the lower grades. "We had what was called a recitation bench," Mrs. Cross said. "One class at a time would come up to the front of the room to the bench and recite a lesson. The others learned from that."

Today, when it is popular to malign and lament the education children are receiving in our elaborate public school systems, it is perhaps ironic to note that as backward as the concept of the one-room schoolhouse seems, it worked. "Everyone learned to read and write," Mrs. Cross emphasized. "And most kids got a good, solid, basic education. No one was lost in the shuffle."

Those sentiments were echoed by Morris Gibber of Kiamesha, who attended a one-room schoolhouse on Fraser Road there in the 1920s. "We received an excellent education," he said. "We learned the basics: reading, writing, and arithmetic, and had to memorize quite a bit too. Each class took turns at the recitation bench, so you had to keep up." About twenty-five students attended grades one through eight in the school full-time, and a few more in the spring and fall when their families moved to the mountains from New York City.

The school was similar in most respects to the ones in which Mrs. Cross taught. "We had a spring nearby from which we carried water in a bucket," Gibber recalled. "Everyone drank from the same dipper. We had a stove to keep warm in the winter, but it seemed you either sat too close to it and roasted or too far from it and froze to death. The older students used to take turns carrying in firewood all winter."

Austin Smith of Barryville, who serves as town of Highland historian, attended school in Eldred from 1916 to 1920. He recalled the building was old even then. "The school was built in 1867," Smith points out. "It was operational until 1960, even after the school district had been centralized. At that time there were only three students left, and they were there only to prove a point: Some residents of the town apparently felt that since the school was created by a vote of the people, only a vote of the people could officially close it, and then only after the board could prove that a central district was cheaper and agreed to turn the schoolhouse into a town hall, which they did."

Smith agrees that the quality of the education students received in the days of the one-room schoolhouse was superior to today's. The difference, he feels, was discipline. "I was not always so well behaved back then," he said. "As punishment, they used to make me stand in the corner. Once, around Christmas, I kept complaining about a cold draft in the corner so the teacher made me sit under the Christmas tree. That was humiliating."

But apparently educational. Perhaps the lesson to be learned is that for all the progress our schools have made in the last few decades, some changes have not necessarily been for the better.

Carriage Makers

ONE does not usually think of Sullivan County in terms of the industry located here, but there was a time when small factories were as common to the county as small hotels would later be. A friend recently pointed out that carriage and wagon manufacturers, for example, were once quite plentiful in the area.

SLICES OF LIFE

"You expressed surprise that there had once been a single toy factory in Monticello," he said, "so you'd probably be overwhelmed by the number of carriage makers who once populated the county."

I decided to check into his contention. I found there were once an extraordinarily large number of carriage and wagon manufacturers in Sullivan County. *Child's Business Directory of 1872-73* listed no fewer than sixty of them, spread out around the county. The more populated communities—Monticello, Mongaup Valley, and Bloomingburgh—had three or four carriage factories each, but almost every town had at least one.

There was the Hortonville Carriage Factory, for instance, owned by Henry Gardner, A. K. Osterhout, and Frederick Fromm. In addition to carriages, they also manufactured wagons and sleighs, and did painting and repairing on the premises.

Staats Lamoreux, who specialized in carriages and sleighs, was located in Liberty. He kept carriages on hand to sell as well as manufactured them to order.

H. S. Romer had just opened a new shop in Sandburgh, which would later become Mountaindale. Romer did all sorts of repairs as well as manufacturing, but "carriage ironing" was his specialty.

Peter Hanyen was a "manufacturer and dealer in heavy and light carriages, wagons, and sleighs," located in Phillipsport.

Josiah Goble had a wagon, carriage and sleigh business on McKee Pond, currently known as Lake Louise Marie. "Two and a half miles east from Bridgeville," his ad stated. "Prepared to do all work in his line in a workman-like manner and from good material. Charges always reasonable. Give us a call and we will satisfy you."

Jacob Faubel of Jeffersonville made "wagons, carriages, and sleighs of all descriptions," and also provided a blacksmith service. "With the best material and experienced workmen, we can do as good work as any shop in the county," his ad claimed.

Edward Heeney was a wagon, carriage and sleigh maker in Glen Wild. He also manufactured and repaired plows, harrows and cultivators.

The Grahamsville Carriage Factory, owned by Daniel Van Keuren, made to order "on short notice, single and double; heavy single and double carriages" as well as wagons, cutters, and sleighs. Spielmann & Peters performed the same function in Youngsville, where they also ran a blacksmith shop. "Satisfaction guaranteed," their ad promised.

Some localities you wouldn't think could have supported a wagon maker actually supported two. Beaver Brook had John Hulse and Hiram Rasseen; Long Eddy had Thomas Livingston and Joseph Miller; Burlingham had Hezekiah Watkins and James Rhinehart, and Wurtsboro had John Howard and Joseph Coddington.

Benjamin and Ira Austin were partners in a wagon-making business in Barryville, R. N. Maben made them in Pike Pond, John Baird in Narrowsburg, and Benjamin Wood in Fremont Center. DeWitt and Johnson were the wagon makers in Woodbourne, John Gorton in Loch Sheldrake, Ira Whipple in Stevensville, and Daniel Bush in Liberty Falls. Thomas Bryan made wagons in Cochecton Center, Peter Theis in Fosterdale, Peter Wall in Beech Wood, and Daniel Hazen in Forestburgh.

Perhaps the most unusual wagon maker of all was in North Branch. Mrs. George Fillweber was not only the lone woman involved in this line of work, she coupled her wagon business with the manufacture and sale of cigars.

Drug Stores Were Fewer, Farther Between

WHEN I WAS GROWING UP in Monticello in the late 1950s and '60s, it seemed like there was a drug store on virtually every block of the village—Aqua's, Spector's, Crain's, Gusar's, Rialto, D'Ari's, to name a few—and I don't think Monticello was unique.

Liberty had at least three—Thompson's, Schiller's, and Klugman's come to mind. Woodridge and South Fallsburg had at least two each, and most other hamlets—Hurleyville, Loch Sheldrake, Wurtsboro, Jeffersonville and Callicoon among them—had at least one.

Such was not always the case. There was a time in the county's history, albeit not recently, when pharmacies—and druggists for that matter—were few and far between. Take 1872, for instance (if for no other reason than that's when Hamilton Child published his comprehensive and authoritative *Gazetteer and Business Directory of Sullivan County*). Child listed only ten drugstores in the entire county, and three of them were in Monticello.

The county seat at that time featured A. B. Crain & Son, perhaps the county's biggest pharmacy, on Main Street. Crain's featured the rather typical fare—"drugs, medicines, and liquors for medicinal purposes"—in addition to merchandise we might consider unconventional for a drug store. Paints, oils, varnishes, putty, glass, dye stuffs, and sewing machines ("The Best, The Cheapest") would fall into this category. Crain's also offered brushes, combs, stationery, fine toilet goods, perfumery, and "a general assortment of various fancy and staple articles. All of good qualities and at reasonable prices."

Charles S. Thornton also had a drugstore and apothecary on Main Street in Monticello. Thornton advertised "drugs, perfumery, patent medicines, toilet and fancy articles" in Child's directory, and promised "physicians' prescriptions carefully compounded." Monticello was also home to W. S. Whitcomb & Company, a pharmacy owned by Winfield S. Whitcomb and E. J. Brown, who referred to themselves as manufacturing chemists.

The only drugstore in Liberty in 1872 was owned by Dr. Alvin Pease, who ran it in conjunction with his dental practice. The store adjoined his dentistry office on Liberty Street, and in addition to drugs, medicines, perfumeries and toilet articles, Dr. Pease also sold "paints, oils, brushes, wall and window paper" as well as lamps and lamp fixtures, and "blank books."

There were only six other drug stores in the county in 1872, and most localities had none within a reasonable distance. Thomas W. Bennett was the pharmacist in Jeffersonville, where he was also a physician and surgeon. Horace W. McKoon dispensed pharmaceuticals in Long Eddy, where, interestingly enough, he also listed himself as a grocer, notary public and farmer. Robert Atkins, the proprietor of the Atkins House hotel in Barryville, served as that hamlet's druggist. Atkins also dealt in groceries.

The three other druggists in Sullivan County in 1872 were all located in the Town of Mamakating. Robert J. Currie operated out of Bloomingburgh, Dr. H. M. Edsall in Wurtsboro—where he was also a physician and surgeon, a lumberman and a farmer—and John L. Knapp in Phillipsport, where he doubled as deputy postmaster.

Of course, things were changing, and in the succeeding decades the number of pharmacists in the county would increase substantially, peaking in the 1950s and '60s. The 1990 Sullivan County Yellow Pages, for instance, lists only seventeen pharmacies in the county, many of them part of large chain stores, and most of them concentrated in Monticello and Liberty.

These listings, of course, don't cover the entire county—sections are served by other phone companies—but it seems safe to say there are fewer than twenty drugstores in Sullivan County today, and with small businesses failing at an alarming rate, we could soon be seeing shades of 1872.

Resort Advertising Reflects Times

SULLIVAN COUNTY has long been known for its resort hotels—local historians believe the first one opened in White Lake in 1811—and famous for the entertainment they provide. During the heyday of the Sullivan County resorts in the late 1920s, hotel entertainment usually consisted of a leisurely game of croquet or badminton, but each hotel owner, facing ever greater competition for the vacationers' dollar, was constantly looking for an edge.

The Flagler, in Old Falls, for example, had been the top dog in hotel entertainment for years, but found itself challenged by Grossinger's and its new social director, Don Hartman, who would later become head of Paramount Pictures. In an attempt to stay one step ahead, the Flagler hired producer Moss Hart as its new social director. Hart brought Dore Schary with him as his assistant. Schary would later become chief of Metro-Goldwyn-Mayer. To go with this impressive duo, the Flagler constructed a new, modern theater elaborate enough to rival those on Broadway.

That's more or less how things remained in Sullivan County for the next few decades. The larger, established hotels featured playhouses or theaters, with live, often big-name entertainment; the smaller hotels relied on casinos. Then, in 1957, the Ambassador Hotel in Old Falls changed all that.

SLICES OF LIFE

The Ambassador constructed the Moulin Rouge, the first real nightclub at a Sullivan County resort. As Manville Wakefield points out in *To the Mountains by Rail*, the opening of the Moulin Rouge began a trend "which would make the old hotel casino obsolete." Indeed, soon the other hotels attempted to keep up with the Ambassador, and by 1958, virtually all the larger hotels in Sullivan County were advertising nightclubs or lounges.

The Flagler responded with the Fiesta Room; Brown's had the Brown Derby; at the Nemerson it was the Penguin Club; at the Raleigh it was simply the Raleigh Room. The Waldemere at Shandalee featured the Oval Room; the Windsor boasted the Calypso Room; the Pines lounge was the Bamboo Room.

And as the competition for tourists heated up, hotels paid more attention to advertising; each one searched for the proper image—just the right words which, whether in a newspaper or magazine or the Yellow Pages, would convince vacationers to stay there. Schenk's touted its "Playhouse of Stars," while the Harmony on Lake Anawana called itself "The big hotel with the homelike atmosphere." The Avon Lodge in Woodridge also boasted a "homelike atmosphere," and claimed "beautiful, natural surroundings." The Pines Hotel opted for "Sullivan County's Paradise," while Brown's called itself "The resort of tomorrow, today!"

Swimming pools. Resorts always featured their swimming pools in their advertising. A pool could be perfuctory (the Windsor), elaborate (the Brown's), exotic (the Pines), or indoor (the Brickman). (Author's collection)

RETROSPECT

The Hotel Gibber in Kiamesha Lake boasted of "fabulous air conditioned buildings," and the Hotel Gradus, just down the road, advertised that it was "fronting beautiful Kiamesha Lake." The Stevensville claimed to be where "vacation plans come true," and the Waldemere called itself "the preferred resort for smart young men and women." The Laurels on Sackett Lake pushed the fact that it had "steam heat throughout," and the Rosemond in Woodridge pointed out it was "overlooking beautiful Silver Lake."

Most of the smaller resorts relied on old advertising staples: playing up their good food, low rates, day camps for children, and golf courses or tennis courts.

All in all, the competition for the vacationer affected not just the hotels, which were forced to improvise and modernize constantly, but the service industries as well. Back then, the hotels spent money in hopes of making money, and the entire county thrived because of it.

The summer resort season in Sullivan County traditionally begins each year on July 4. But for the prospective tourist, planning for that resort season begins much earlier in the year. In past seasons, city residents planning to summer in the Catskills usually started evaluating potential resorts shortly after the arrival of spring. For many years, the primary tool in that evaluation process was the Vacation Guide printed by the Ontario and Western Railway.

Railroad stations. During the early days of the Sullivan County resort boom, tourists arrived via the Ontario & Western Railway, which entered the county in Bloomingburgh and continued northwesterly to Roscoe. (Author's collection)

The O&W guide was a small booklet designed to introduce the neophyte tourist to the potential delights of destinations along the route of the railroad. Actually, very little of the booklet was devoted to editorial space; most was taken up with paid advertisements by the dozens of resorts in the area the booklet covered.

SLICES OF LIFE

I recently came across a 1949 edition of the guide that covered Sullivan, Ulster, Orange, and Delaware Counties, and I was amazed and saddened by the number of hotels advertising there that no longer exist. Some are deserted skeletons, burned out or simply dilapidated; others have disappeared completely, living on only in the memories of a few.

The vacation guide traced the route of the railroad through the county, and most of the advertising followed suit. Therefore, the Sha-Wan-Ga Lodge in High View was the first Sullivan County resort one came across, its three-page ad boasting, "something doing every minute for those who want sport and action." The Hotel Ambassador in Fallsburg was next, boasting "collegiate basketball, large filtered sulfur water pool, tennis courts, new baseball field, commodious recreation hall, top-talent entertainment nightly, and a children's day camp." The Ambassador ad also touted the opening of the hotel's new rendezvous, The Embassy Room.

The Hotel Furst invited the prospective tourist to "join in on the fun & frolic" in its small ad. The ad highlighted the hotel's "comfortable, airy, modern rooms," and boasted "every summer sport." The River View in South Fallsburg was next. Its ad was nearly a half page, and promised a "friendly, congenial resort" with "all sports, moderate rates, excellent cuisine, dancing, entertainment" and a children's day camp.

The Nemerson and the Plaza, two South Fallsburg hotels, both took out full-page ads in the guide. The Nemerson stressed its new Rainbow Room, "a smart, inviting rendezvous for a cocktail...late night get-together...Latin American rhythms...intimate entertainment and dancing until 3:00 a.m." The Plaza, on the other hand, listed "elevator service" among its features—the only hotel in the guide to do so—and pointed to its new filtered swimming pool. The Plaza was "in a class by itself," the ad promised.

The Flagler Hotel and Country Club also ran a full-page ad, promising "professional instructors in all games and sports" and listed among the sports it offered something called "aquatics." The Flagler boasted a fireproof sprinkler system and steam heat in every room.

The Gibbers in Kiamesha Lake built its ad around "our feature—meals to write home about" and highlighted its Walnut Room, and separate kosher kitchen. The Hotel Levbourne in Woodbourne had a "splendid 150-acre park, safe and away from traffic" and offered a rhumba dance band. The Columbia Hotel in Hurleyville pushed its "unexcelled cuisine" and "fresh vegetables from our farm," as well as "hot and cold running water in every room."

"All this and nature too!" screamed the half-page ad for Brown's. New for 1949, according to the hotel's ad, was the Brown Derby night club, a spacious social hall, a cocktail lounge, and canteen. The Hotel Evans in Loch Sheldrake had a two-page ad that challenged the tourist to uncover "the ultimate in vacation happiness." The Evans had just completed a new forty-acre lake "centered with an enchanting island which consists of a lavish night club, fire places, and a recreation room." The hotel's new building, the Governor, featured private baths and showers in every room.

Among the lesser-known resorts advertising in the Vacation Guide was the Crispell Farm resort in Ferndale. This converted farmhouse featured "all modern improvements," including "comfortable beds, inner spring mattresses, hot and cold running water, nice large dining room, individual small tables, and milk from tuberculin tested cows."

Tourists opting for a less-sedentary time were invited to "leap into summer fun" at Ferndale's Lakeside Inn and Country Club. "Every day a thrilling day," the Lakeside's ad promised.

Grossinger's was featured in a two-page spread in the booklet. The background of the ad was a cloudless sky, with graphics, provided by two sky-writing planes, boasting, "Grossinger's has everything." Specifically, the ad noted a new "super-pool, a championship 18 hole golf course, private stables and riding trails, the famous Terrace Room, and the completely equipped new Grossinger Airport."

The Lesser Lodge in White Sulphur Springs was featured in a half-page ad which promised "regulation tennis, hand-ball, and basketball courts, baseball field, fishing, golf, and saddle horses in the immediate vicinity." The Horseshoe Lake House in Bethel also purchased a half-page ad in the booklet. The ad promised "a homelike hotel" on an estate of 500 acres with a large private natural lake and a sandy beach for swimming.

Klein's Hillside in Parksville ran a full-page ad that promoted, among other things, the resort's superb athletic facilities. "Acclaimed far and wide as the perfect play-ground, Klein's holds more in store this year than ever before," the ad boasted. "Now experience a real thrill, rowing on our scenic lake." Prospective tourists were reminded in a full-page ad that at the Lash Hotel in Parksville, "your vacation becomes an adventure."

A number of Livingston Manor resorts advertised in the guide, including the Beaver Lake Lodge, the Trojan Lake Lodge, the White Roe, and the Parkston, which took a two-page ad obviously aimed at the younger tourists: "Young people say it's the Parkston for vacation value," the ad boasted.

The Sunrise in Livingston Manor took that philosophy one step further, calling itself "the leading hotel for young folks only" in its own two-page spread. The ad promised, in what must be the ultimate in narrow demographic targeting, that "Honeymooners will find the Sunrise Hotel an ideal location for a perfect honeymoon. Located in the most beautiful spot in Livingston Manor, and with activities and social events going on at all times, you are bound to remember a Sunrise Honeymoon in June."

The Waldemere Hotel was a third Livingston Manor resort running a two-page advertisement. The hotel chose to highlight its "splendid Hungarian cuisine," its "newly built macadam road direct to the hotel," and its "smart new nite club featuring the tops in Rhumba rhythms."

The Sullivan County section of the Vacation Guide was closed out, perhaps fittingly, by a full-page ad for the combined villages of Roscoe-Rockland, which billed itself then not as "the last frontier," but as "where the Kodak trail begins."

There were over 325 hotels in Sullivan County in 1958. By 1988, there were fewer than 100, many of them motels. Perhaps that, more than anything, illustrates the changes the county has undergone in the intervening years.

RETROSPECT

Old Remedies, Lawyers and Cheap Coffins

I SUPPOSE I have always been interested in old newspapers. I recently had the good fortune to come into possession of some and, after catching up on the news, I had a field day reading the ads.

I found some of the advertisements in a Dec. 2, 1859, issue of the Monticello *Jeffersonian Democrat* particularly eye-catching. The *Jeffersonian Democrat* was published by Reynolds and Matthews in offices over Piercy's Drug Store in the village. Advertising cost fifty cents for twenty lines or less in 1859, and a year's subscription was $1. The paper was dominated by ads for medicines and formulas guaranteed to cure everything from consumption to scurvy.

One ad hawked Dr. Mott's Chalybeate Pills, "an aperient and stomachic preparation of iron purified of oxygen and carbon by combustion in hydrogen, of high medical authority and extraordinary efficacy in a number of complaints, including debility, emaciations, dyspepsia, diarrhea, constipation, scrofula, female weakness and mismenstruation."

Another ad touted Dr. Churchill's Remedy, "a genuine preparation of hypophosphites of lime and soda," which was supposed to cure and prevent consumption. "The hypophosphites increase the principle which constitutes nervous force and are the most powerful blood generating agents known," the ad claimed.

Of course, medicine wasn't all that was advertised. One ad pointed out that "Miss Melissa Voorhes has just opened a new millinery at Joscelynville where she will keep constantly on hand a large and handsome stock of goods."

George Watts, a plumber and painter, advertised in the *Jeffersonian Democrat*, as did Watkins & Kilbourn, a general merchandise store in Liberty. So did the Woodbourne House Hotel and D. M. Stewart, a manufacturer and wholesaler of boots and shoes.

No fewer that eight different law offices advertised, including John G. Childs of Neversink; L. Anderson of Jeffersonville; H. Shaver of Callicoon Depot; Robert Tillotson of Mongaup Valley; Albert J. Bush of Parksville; and James Matthews, Henry R. Low, and partners J. L. Stewart and W. J. Groo, of Monticello.

SLICES OF LIFE

O. A. Carroll, a physician and surgeon with offices "opposite the Watchman office" in Monticello, promised prompt attendance to all calls in his ad.

L. A. Ketchum, a jeweler, advertised a special on watch repairing. His price for cleaning levers, for example, had been reduced from eight shillings to seventy-five cents; for replacing the main spring from twelve shillings to seventy-five cents, and for replacing the crystal from two shillings to twelve cents. Nathan Stern of Monticello had a sale on remnants. His calico, which normally sold for ten cents, was being offered for six; bleached muslin could be had for ten cents a yard; ginghams, normally sold for sixteen cents, were reduced to eleven cents; and wool flannels were reduced from fifty to thirty-four cents.

William Mitchell of Monticello advertised bargains in furniture, including sofas, rockers, easy chairs, bureaus, and cheap coffins. "Come and buy your furniture of me, and you will go away rejoicing," his ad promised.

Though now we're used to one-stop shopping at a mall or "super" stores, in days gone by shopping was done in much smaller, simpler neighborhood stores.

Take Hammond & Cooke in Monticello, for instance. This fine clothing store occupied the same Broadway location for over half a century. The owners always prided themselves on offering quality merchandise at competitive prices. In a 1919 advertisement in the *Republican Watchman*, Hammond & Cooke was touting a "pre-inventory" sale, in which they offered "all our ladies coats and suits at big reductions."

"Now is the time to buy a nice suit or coat," the ad urges, and goes on to list a number of coats at significant reductions. Coats that normally sold for $50 were being offered for $38.50; those normally priced $45 were on sale for $35; coats which usually sold for $35 were offered for $25; and those typically priced $28.50 were marked down to $22.50. Everyday $25 coats were selling for $20, while those normally selling for $20 were $16.50, and those normally $15 were just $10. All ladies' suits were on sale, and ladies' silk and serge dresses were also offered at big reductions.

Hammond & Cooke also offered men's overcoats from $10 to $40, men's fur coats from $15 to $35, men's fur-lined coats from $30 to $50, and sheep-lined coats at $13 to $30.

The *Watchman* had the largest circulation of any newspaper in Sullivan County in 1919, and just about everyone advertised within its pages. It was published in Monticello by Adelbert Scriber. Its other ads included John J. Burns' Department Store at 238-240 Broadway, which also advertised men's overcoats. "Now is the time you will get a full winter's wear out of them," the ad reminded.

B. Fishman advertised his Monticello Variety Store at 302 Broadway in that *Watchman*, too. The store offered an "extensive line of crockery, agate, tinware, and other articles," as well as a "full line of dry goods, such as underwear, dresses, skirts, waists, corsets, hosiery, and piece goods." The Monticello Variety Store also carried a "big variety of ladies, men's and children's sweaters," souvenirs, and toys.

The Arcade Theater announced it was operating under new management, and would be offering "the best pictures obtainable, regardless of cost." The ad promised "Only high grade pictures will be shown."

Electrician A. J. Pantel of South Fallsburg advertised "Delco-Light" the complete electric light and power plant. "Pumps the water and grinds the feed," the ad said. "An extra hand at chore time."

McLaughlin Brothers Insurance and Real Estate office, located in the Masonic Building in Monticello, advertised in the *Watchman*, as did its competitor, Hornbeck & Calkin, located in the Bank Building.

Doctor R. J. Schreiber advertised his veterinary practice, F. L. Stratton and Lamont Mitchell their undertaking businesses, and Edward Holden his real estate office. Bishop & Avery offered artesian wells, Philip Krukin solicited business for his optician's practice, and Dr. Floyd Cook of Middletown pointed out that he held office hours until 4 p.m. daily except Friday.

As usual, the paper's remaining ad space was devoted to medicines and formulas designed to alleviate a number of ailments. These included Scott's Emulsion, which warmed children and adults who suffered from cold hands and feet; Schiffman's Catarrh Balm, for hay fever; Parker's Hair Balsam, for restoring color and beauty to gray hair; and Asthmador, an instant relief for asthma.

SLICES OF LIFE

Marrianne Reed, of Liberty, sent me an issue of the *Republican Watchman* dated May 18, 1917. Most of the news stories in that issue revolved around America's role in World War I, including one which pointed out that the first war bill was over $3.3 billion.

But it was the advertising which I spent the most time reading. I found the classified ads in this particular issue especially interesting. As might be expected, one could find just about anything one might be looking for, and then some—from cars for hire to cars for sale, from farms for rent to a boarding house offered "for exchange."

Consider these help wanted ads:

GIRL WANTED: for light housework and as companion; one in family, no washing. Apply E. Chant, 43 St. John Street, Monticello.
WANTED: cook and woman for general work and girls for chambermaids and waitresses. B. LaTourette, Monticello.
WANTED: Good man to work on farm; good heavy work horse, sulky plow, sulky two-row cultivator; also have some oat and rye straw for sale. Address Floyd Pelton, Monticello.
SALESMAN WANTED: Lubricating oil, grease, specialties, paint. Part or whole time. Commission basis until ability established. Man with rig preferred. Riverside Refining Company, Cleveland, Ohio.

While ads similar to these might be found in any newspaper today, subtle nuances give us an idea that things were just a bit different in 1917:

FOR SALE: 1916 touring car, fully equipped, demountable rims, brand new tires, machine in good condition. Goes to first cash buyer. Can be seen at Geraghty's Garage, Monticello.
1917 CAR FOR HIRE: Will go anywhere at anytime. Rates reasonable. Will meet any Fallsburgh [sic] train. Jack Taylor, Phone 45-J or 49-M.
AUTOMOBILE FOR SALE: Seven passenger, six-cylinder Mitchell, in good condition with good tires. An unusual bargain at $450. Richard Harms, Monticello.

RETROSPECT

NORWAY SPRUCE TREES FOR SALE: Nursery grown at Kiamesha. Five young, quick growing ornamental evergreens, 50 cents each. Three to four feet high. Wm. Bengough, Kiamesha.

Music Lessons: 25 cents per lesson. I am organizing a class of beginners. It is important to begin right. Call at my home, 317 Broadway, at 4 o'clock. Carolyn M. Scriber.

ANTHONY METZGER OF LIBERTY will include Monticello this summer as part of his territory to do expert piano tuning and repairing. Uprights $2.50, Grands $3.

PIGS FOR SALE: Chester White, 5 weeks old, $5 apiece. Telephone 117-F2. Rosemary Farm.

WAR BOOK: History of 10th Legion for $2. Every Sullivan County family should have a copy. Judge Joel Fisk, Liberty.

FARM FOR SALE: White Lake village. 88 acres, fine orchard, two furnished houses, barn, outbuildings, three blocks from lake. Price $8,000. Easy terms, will rent. E. B. Crawford, Mast Hope, Pa.

Steam heated flat for rent: $12 per month. Inquire Watchman office.

FOR SALE OR EXCHANGE: Boarding house with store, large hall and farm in Bethel village, 60 acres grass farm near White Lake and 18 acres building lots near Monticello. Easy terms. Box 33, Bethel.

Now, honestly, when was the last time you saw a farm for sale for $8,000, an apartment to rent for $12 a month, or a property offered for exchange? Things like that just don't appear in today's classifieds.

Nothing better reflects the lifestyle of the times, I've found, than the newspaper ads. I was given a number of old newspapers from the late 1940s, including the *Bulletin-Sentinel* (the weekly paper formed from the merger of the Monticello *Bulletin* and the Hurleyville *Sentinel*) and the *Evening News* (the only daily newspaper ever published in Sullivan County), and I was surprised at the number of restaurant ads appearing in them.

Whether it was the post-war boom or something else, Americans seemed to embark on an eating-out trend in the late '40s that is still going strong, and if the advertisements in these papers are any indication, Sullivan County was right in the midst of that trend.

SLICES OF LIFE

The March 19, 1946, edition of the *Bulletin-Sentinel* featured a fairly large ad for The Paddock restaurant "on Route 17—one mile east of Monticello." The Paddock called itself "the show place of the mountains" and boasted "fine foods served in fine manner in a fine atmosphere." "Our new exquisite Tack Lounge is now open" the ad announced, promoting "music during your meal by Jerry Altess and Ben Macomber on the Hammond Electric Novacord."

For those preferring Chinese food, there was The Brown Front Bar & Grill at 294 Broadway in Monticello. The Brown Front, "where good fellowship reigns supreme," prided itself on genuine chow mein and chop suey, served daily under the supervision of Fin Lee, "expert in preparing oriental dishes." Chili con carne and Italian spaghetti were also available at the Brown Front, as was "a bar with one price for all."

The Log Cabin Bar & Grill at 289 Broadway in Monticello, a "comfortable and spacious cafe," offering choice refreshments and sandwiches, and Klein's Bar & Grill, featuring "good food and drinks" also advertised in this edition of the paper, though the latter grill neglected to include its address.

If the March 17, 1947, edition of the *Evening News* is any indication, the dining-out trend hadn't abated any the next year. Leon & Chezzy's Bar & Grill on Kiamesha Lake, under new management, advertised its "delicious steaks" and promised "special attention to parties." Ernie's Bar & Grill in Hurleyville boasted "always a good time" and advertised its Chinese food and "all kinds of sandwiches."

Peppy's, "on Route 17, two miles below Monticello," chose to spotlight its turkey and shrimp, and pointed out that there was "dancing every Saturday night to music by Buffee Dee and his orchestra." The Park Restaurant on Broadway in Monticello claimed "always the finest foods and choicest liquors in pleasant surroundings," and touted its seafood specialties. Solly Legon's had by this time replaced the Brown Front at 294 Broadway, and had imported Hong Tong to prepare "Chinese dishes of all descriptions." The specialties included lobster Cantonese, spare ribs, egg rolls, and roast pork.

It was more of the same in the October 28, 1947 issue of the *Bulletin-Sentinel*. Visco's Restaurant, a White Lake eatery specializing in Italian cuisine, advertised its Pine Room, where Elmer King called square dances every Saturday night to the music of the Sod Busters. Also advertising was Pat Visco's New Jefferson Hotel Bar and Restaurant on Jefferson Street in Monticello, "where food and service are always at the height of perfection." The New Jefferson Hotel featured "the finest in Italian and American food."

The May 11, 1948 *Bulletin-Sentinel* included the announcement that the Columbia Farm-Hotel in Hurleyville was opening for Sunday dinner from 1 to 3:30 pm and for supper from 6 to 7:30. The Columbia Farm ad also announced that there would be dancing every Saturday night after May 15, an apparent indication that business was quite seasonal in Sullivan County, even back then.

Year of the Great Sesquicentennial

THE YEAR 1954 was truly significant for the village of Monticello: It not only marked the 150th anniversary of the founding of the village, but it was the year of perhaps the biggest event ever in the community—the celebration of that sesquicentennial.

The Monticello Sesquicentennial Celebration took place over five days in 1954, September 7 through 11, and included two parades, a Sesquicentennial Ball, the crowning of a Sesquicentennial Queen, and a huge pageant featuring a cast of nearly 400. The preparations for the five-day spectacle took almost a year.

Don Hammond and Manny Bogner were co-chairs of the Sesquicentennial Committee, and were primarily responsible for the smoothness with which the huge celebration was conducted. What made the spectacle such an overwhelming success, however, was the enthusiastic involvement of the entire community. The event became so significant, in fact, that it was read about in London, Paris, and Rome, and photos connected with the celebration were run in newspapers from Atlanta to Minneapolis.

"It was quite simply the greatest thing that ever happened in this community," Don Hammond remembered. "Everybody worked on it. What made it a success was that the whole community got involved."

If Hammond and Bogner were the movers and the shakers behind the celebration, it was an outsider who really put it all together.

SLICES OF LIFE

Edmund Nejaimey was an employee of the John B. Rogers Production Company of Fosteria, Ohio, the firm hired by the Sesquicentennial Committee to assist in organizing the celebration. "He came to town around June," Hammond recalled. "From that point on, he masterminded the whole thing. But we all put a lot of work into it. It was a consuming thing."

An historical spectacle, which was produced for four nights at the Monticello Airport, told the story of the founding of Monticello by John Patterson Jones in 1804. It did so in fifteen episodes, each of which told a story from the village's past, from its beginning through the early 1900s. Nearly 400 citizens were in the cast, and hundreds of others assisted in other ways.

"They had to close the field down for a week to get it ready. We constructed bleachers for viewing, and a huge stage. It was quite a sight," Hammond said. A chorus of about sixty voices provided the background music, while other village residents served on committees overseeing decorations, props, parking, concessions and the like.

But none of the aspects of the Sesquicentennial Celebration generated as much publicity as the Brothers of the Brush organization. A proclamation proposed by that group and adopted by the village board led to news of the Monticello celebration the world over. Even a contender for the world's heavyweight boxing championship eventually got involved.

"We got the idea that all men in the village should grow beards as part of the sesquicentennial," recalled Hammond. "We formed a group called Brothers of the Brush, and we charged each man a dollar for the privilege of joining— actually, for the privilege of growing a beard." Few, if any, groups ever created the furor the Monticello Brothers of the Brush managed.

"The mayor of the village, Samuel Sprayregan, declared that after Easter Sunday it would be a violation to shave. All the men were to put their razors away after that day," Hammond said. What followed were storms of protest, first from the village's Master Barber's Association, and eventually from the female population.

"I represented the Master Barber's Association," Monticello attorney Jacob Acks said. "Max Racker was the president of the group and Foster Little was the secretary. We filed a motion that asked that the declaration that all men must grow beards be set aside, since it was hurting the barber's business." The motion was denied by Justice of the Peace Morris Rosenbloom, who felt the barbers would more than make up for their lost business after the celebration, when the beards would come off.

So, the declaration stood, and all the males in the village were required to grow beards. Those who did not were hauled before a kangaroo court and fined.

Even heavyweight boxing great Ezzard Charles, training at Kutsher's Country Club for a championship clash with Rocky Marciano, grew a beard. "It was all done to generate publicity for the sesquicentennial," Acks admitted. "We felt it would focus attention on the celebration."

And that it did. Stories of the village beards appeared in newspapers throughout the region and in New York City. About a hundred women, led by Estelle Shulman and Ann Kaplan, picketed the Sesquicentennial Committee's office on Broadway, placards in hand. They claimed that the men's beards were making their lives miserable. Mrs. Shulman and Mrs. Kaplan were arrested; a photograph of the arrest was picked up by the United Press International and eventually appeared in hundreds of newspapers throughout the country, including the *Atlanta Journal*, the *Cincinnati Inquirer* and the *Minneapolis Tribune*. Accounts of the protest, the arrests, and the subsequent hearing and trial were carried internationally by papers in Rome, Paris and London.

Mayor Sprayregan made one of the most auspicious sacrifices, as newspaper accounts related the sad tale of the plight he suffered for obeying the law. His wife was so disgusted by his beard, the articles read, that she locked him out of the house for the duration and he had to live in a local hotel.

Nothing like the 1954 Monticello Sesquicentennial Celebration has ever taken place since, nor is it likely to. "The character of the community has changed too much," Hammond said. "I doubt it could ever happen again. Maybe we'll find out when the Bicentennial rolls around in 2004."

Chapter 5

Entertainment

Mongaup, Movies and Murder

A FAMOUS STARLET, a Hollywood director, and a seventy-year-old unsolved murder—just the kind of thing any red-blooded American loves to read about. Throw in a link to a well-known Sullivan County landmark, and it quickly becomes a story I can't resist telling.

I'm sure Ed Van Put had no idea when he sent me the newspaper clipping that started me on the trail of this intriguing story just how compelling I would find it. The clipping, taken from the February 18, 1922 Walton *Reporter*, arrived in the mail with a note from Van Put. "Something I thought you would like to see," the Livingston Manor man wrote. The article read:

> William Desmond Taylor, the prominent moving picture director who was murdered in his Los Angeles apartments a few days ago, by an assassin who shot him in the back of the head with a revolver, created a sensation in this section in September, 1920, when he brought a troupe of movie actors to Sullivan County to find a fitting setting for one of the productions that later became prominent.
>
> Taylor found the place he was looking for at Mongaup Falls, a few miles from Monticello, and with his small army of movie people spent several days there in completing the picture, 'Anna of Green Gables.' Mary Miles Minter was featured in the Mongaup Falls production.

I was familiar with the magnificent beauty of Mongaup Falls, destroyed by a utility company in 1923, but I wasn't aware that it had once been used as the setting for a motion picture. I was curious to know more about the film, its director, and its star.

The film was actually titled *Anne of Green Gables* and was released by Paramount in 1919. This would seem to indicate that the filming at Mongaup Falls took place in 1918 or 1919, but certainly not in 1920. Those inaccuracies aside, the murder of director William Desmond Taylor to which the clipping referred, and the involvement of actress Mary Miles Minter in that murder, make an especially interesting story.

The film was based on the book of the same name by L. M. Montgomery. It depicted the misadventures of a young orphan girl who is living with her uncle and his unmarried sister at their country home, Green Gables. Minter, a former child star (she began acting at the age of four) who resembled Mary Pickford, had the title role in the film, the first of four in which she would collaborate with director Taylor.

Ironically, it was this collaboration which would lead to Minter's tragic downfall and, in all probability, contribute to Taylor's untimely death just a few years later.

Prior to his murder, the forty-five-year-old Taylor had been romantically linked to a number of Hollywood ladies, including well-known comedienne Mabel Normand. Normand, in fact, became the first suspect in the director's death. But the discovery among his personal effects of a love letter from the twenty-one-year-old Minter changed all that. Although it was speculated that a scorned and enraged Minter had shot and killed the man she loved, police could never prove it.

The murder and the love triangle the ensuing investigation revealed was played up in the tabloids of the day, and the resulting publicity was enough to ruin Minter's career—the scandal-sensitive public would no longer pay to see her perform. She made only four films after Taylor's death, none of them notable.

It is inconceivable that someone whose career once seemed so promising—Minter earned over a million dollars as a silent-screen star—is today best remembered for her suspected role in a murder, but such was her fate. She never recovered—professionally or emotionally—from Taylor's death, and the case continued to hound her for decades. When a 1970s television show examined the mysterious murder, implying that Minter was one of three women who could have killed Taylor (her jealous mother and Normand were presumably the others), Minter sued for invasion of privacy. She lost.

Minter's work in *Anne of Green Gables* is generally considered among her finest, and it is that film which connects the curly-haired actress—and Taylor—to this area, and forever serves as a link between Sullivan County and one of Hollywood's most enduring scandals.

Caesar Gets Votes for Comedy Hall of Fame

AN ENTERTAINMENT HALL OF FAME AND MUSEUM—immortalizing the distinctive humor of the Borscht Belt—has people talking. They're talking about the possible economic benefits the establishment and its spin-offs might provide to the area. They're talking about the nationwide attention it will bring Sullivan County. And they're talking about the stars who will likely be enshrined there.

Sid Caesar is one whose name has come up in a number of conversations. Caesar, most known for his four-year stint on the early television hit, *Your Show of Shows*, spent years in the Catskills working as the resident comic at the Avon Lodge in Woodridge.

But his ties to the area go back further than that. He started his entertainment career in 1936 as a kid saxophonist—he was only fourteen—playing for the summer at the Hotel Anderson on Old Liberty Road outside Monticello. There, he told *International Jewish Monthly* magazine, he often filled in as a stooge for the hotel's regular burlesque comedian. It was an inauspicious introduction to the world of Catskill resorts: The Anderson—despite the slot machines found in its lobby—was not among the swankiest spots.

Still, the experience Caesar gained working the summer crowds proved invaluable. He became a full-time musician—sort of—after graduating high school. In between irregular gigs with New York City bands, he ushered at the Capitol Theatre, and he continued to work summers here in the mountains. In fact, it was during those years, roughly between 1939 and 1941, that he developed his trademark improvisational comedy sketches. The work apparently paid off, because in 1942 he became the resident comic at the Avon. He would shortly thereafter marry the hotel owner's niece.

His Catskill career was interrupted by a stint in the Coast Guard, but the reputation he had built landed him guest shots on Milton Berle's new television show in 1948, and in January 1949 he kicked off the *Admiral Broadway Revue* with Imogene Coca. This short-lived variety show, which dominated Friday-night programming the way Berle did Tuesday night and Ed Sullivan did Sunday night, was one of the few major programs ever to be carried by two networks simultaneously—it aired on both NBC and the DuMont network from 8 to 9 pm.

Although the *Admiral Broadway Revue* lasted just six months, it was significant in that it paired Caesar and Coca for the first time. Just six months after the *Revue* folded, the duo reunited in *Your Show of Shows*. This classic of television's golden age ran for four years and spawned the careers of a number of successful comedy writers, including Mel Brooks, Neil Simon, Woody Allen, and Larry Gelbart. The show also featured the comedy of Carl Reiner and Howard Morris—but Caesar and Coca were the indisputable stars, creating such immortal characters as the husband-and-wife Hickenloopers.

Your Show of Shows was still going strong when Caesar and Coca decided to pursue separate solo careers in 1954. For him, that meant the comedy-variety show *Caesar's Hour* on NBC. Reiner and Morris accompanied Caesar in the new format, but despite the added comedic talents of regulars Nanette Fabray and Pat Carroll, *Caesar's Hour* never approached the success of *Your Show of Shows*. Still, it managed a three-year run on NBC, and gave America the hilarious sketch, "The Commuters," in which Caesar, Reiner, and Morris portrayed suburbanites who take the same train to work every morning and the same train home each evening.

For Sid Caesar, television comedy was a far cry from his days of playing the saxophone at the Hotel Anderson outside Monticello. He had become a legend—as have other entertainers with indisputable links to Sullivan County, including Jerry Lewis, Buddy Hackett, Danny Kaye, Moss Hart, Irving Berlin, Sammy Fain, and Dore Schary.

ENTERTAINMENT

Of Berlin and Fain, much has been written; Hart and Schary are probably somewhat more obscure. Take Hart, for instance: He came to the Flagler in 1929, largely because the hotel, for years the unchallenged king of the mountains, was feeling the pressure of competition from Grossinger's and its impressive social director, Don Hartman, a man who would one day screenwrite many of the "road" pictures for Bob Hope and Bing Crosby; he'd later head up Paramount Pictures.

Hart almost immediately hired Schary as his assistant; together, their tenure was short but productive. Teaming up for productions in the resort's new, state-of-the-art playhouse, they kept the Flagler on top of the hotel heap for a few more years.

The Flagler's star might have been on the decline by the early 1930s, but Hart's had just begun to rise. He co-wrote the play *Once in a Lifetime* with George S. Kaufman in 1932, and when Universal turned the story of how a script is sold in Hollywood into a Jack Oakie movie a year later, Hart had arrived on the threshold of the big-time. He followed that success with *The Man Who Came to Dinner*, which was turned into a movie with Monty Wooley and Bette Davis in 1941.

In 1944, he wrote both the play and the screen adaptation of *Winged Victory*, and in 1947 was nominated for an Academy Award for his screenplay *Gentleman's Agreement*, which was selected as "Best Picture" that year. Other notable Hart screenplays included Danny Kaye's *Hans Christian Andersen* in 1952, and the Judy Garland version of *A Star is Born* in 1954.

Hart was only 57 when he died in 1961. His autobiography, *Act One*, was made into a movie in 1963, with George Hamilton in the lead role.

Ironically, it was Schary, Hart's erstwhile assistant, who wrote the screenplay and directed the film. By that time, Schary had already built himself a name in Hollywood that had surpassed even Hart's. In 1938, he had won an Academy Award for co-writing the screenplay for the movie *Boys Town*, with Spencer Tracy and Mickey Rooney. He became a producer for Metro-Goldwyn-Mayer from 1941 to 1945, and then head of production at RKO from '45 to '48.

He returned to MGM as head of production in 1948, and lasted in that relatively thankless job until 1956, despite failing to pick up on the latent talents of an aspiring young actress named Marilyn Monroe. After leaving MGM, Schary wrote independently for a time, his most notable success being the critically acclaimed life story of Franklin Roosevelt, *Sunrise at Campobello*, which he wrote for the stage and later adapted to the big screen. Through it all, he regarded fame as fleeting and fickle.

"Show business is a high and incredible lottery, a fantastic dice game, a mammoth roulette wheel," he wrote in *The Atlantic* in October 1959. Schary published his autobiography, *Heyday*, in 1979 and died a year later at the age of 75.

Both Hart and Schary departed the Catskills before they achieved their considerable fame; neither left what might be considered an indelible mark on the mountains. But who can deny that the experience they gained while putting together the elaborate shows at the Flagler was invaluable to their respective careers?

And what about Sammy Fain?

Sammy *who*?

That so few people are aware of Sammy Fain's considerable accomplishments is unfair. He's best known for the songs "Secret Love" (from the 1953 Doris Day/Howard Keel movie *Calamity Jane*) and "Love Is a Many Splendored Thing" (from the 1955 film of the same name with William Holden and Jennifer Jones) on which he collaborated with lyricist Paul Francis Webster, and for which he won Academy Awards. But his song writing credits didn't stop there.

He also penned such classics as "I'll Be Seeing You" and "I Can Dream, Can't I," both popular during World War II—the latter a major hit for the Andrews Sisters. Other Fain standards include "Let a Smile Be Your Umbrella," "Wedding Bells Are Breaking Up That Old Gang of Mine," and "Tender Is the Night."

Fain certainly had more direct ties to the area than Hart, Schary, or even Berlin. He was born in 1902 on New York's Lower East Side. His father, Abraham Feinberg, was a cantor in the neighborhood synagogue. The family moved to South Fallsburg when Sammy was about three years old.

By all accounts, Fain began composing songs at an early age, despite the fact that he never had any formal training reading music; in fact, there was some speculation that he never learned to read music at all. Even after he had gained a certain measure of success, he used to try out many of his tunes at his family's small hotel, the Fain Lodge, on Route 42 in South Fallsburg. He would play the piano while his brother Harry entertained on the violin. The resort could not have contracted for such top-notch entertainment had it tried.

The hotel was sold shortly after Fain's parents died in the 1940s, but relatives later bought the nearby home where the family had lived. Fain himself lived in South Fallsburg until the early 1930s, and frequently returned to visit his numerous relatives there. One such trip included his being honored at a local celebrity night at Monticello Raceway in the 1970s.

Shortly after leaving South Fallsburg in search of fame and fortune in the world of show business, Fain began working in Hollywood musicals, beginning in 1933 with the Busby Berkeley production, *Footlight Parade,* with James Cagney, Joan Blondell, Dick Powell and Ruby Keeler. In 1935, he worked on *Dames* with Blondell, Powell, and Keeler, and *Going to Town,* Mae West's last movie effort before Hollywood censors took the bite out of her act. Other Hollywood credits included *Alice In Wonderland* and *Peter Pan.* On Broadway, Fain worked on the 1938 revue, *Hellzapoppin,* and other lesser-known productions.

Sammy Fain died in Los Angeles on Dec. 6, 1989. He was 87. For all his success, upon his death he was remembered at least as much for being "a warm, loving, caring fellow" as for being a successful songwriter.

Berlin's Local Legacy

JEROME KERN once said, "Irving Berlin has no place in American music. He *is* American music."

The man who gave us such classics as "White Christmas" and "God Bless America," spent much of the last sixty years of his life here in Sullivan County.

Irving Berlin was born in Russia in 1888—his real name was Israel Baline—and came to America with his family when he was five. They settled on New York City's Lower East Side, where young Israel helped his cantor father support the family by singing on the street corner for handouts. Things got worse financially when his father died and, at the age of twelve, Israel was forced to take a job as a singing waiter in a run-down Chinatown tourist trap. The youngster had a natural knack for composing bawdy parodies of well-known songs; it was an ability that made him particularly popular with the cafe's rough-and-tumble patrons.

The squalor of his early life notwithstanding, Berlin seemed destined for greatness. He wrote music and lyrics with equal skill, and following some successful work on Broadway began to work on Hollywood films, as well. His first film of note was a 1928 effort, *The Awakening*, and he followed that a year later by providing the music and lyrics for the Paramount picture *The Coconuts*, which introduced a four-brother comedy team called the Marx Brothers.

The 1930s brought some of Berlin's biggest hits, including *Top Hat*, with Fred Astaire and Ginger Rogers (for which his song, "Cheek to Cheek" received an Oscar nomination); *Follow the Fleet*, with Astaire, Rogers, Randolph Scott and Harriet Hilliard; and *Alexander's Ragtime Band*, with Tyrone Power, Alice Faye, and Ethel Merman ("Now it Can Be Told," one of the twenty-six songs Berlin composed for *Alexander's Ragtime Band*, got him his second Oscar nomination).

It was during this decade that Berlin moved his family to Sullivan County for the summer. He had a home built in Lew Beach; the family stayed at the nearby Edgewood Inn while the house was being constructed. They would spend considerable time in the area during the next fifty-odd years, but rarely socialized. While in Sullivan County, Berlin would travel mainly by chauffeur-driven limousine, and rarely at that. He is remembered as a man who insisted upon privacy, but was generous and gracious to those with whom he dealt. He told interviewers that he enjoyed the mountains of Sullivan County because of the fresh air they provided and because they reminded him of pictures he had seen of his birthplace in Russia.

His success continued—in fact, burgeoned—in the 1940s, during which time he worked on a number of top-notch movies, including *This Is the Army* (in which he also appeared, singing, "How I Hate To Get Up in The Morning"); the Fred Astaire/Bing Crosby film, *Blue Skies* (for which Berlin's "You Keep Coming Back Like a Song" was nominated for an Academy Award); *Easter Parade*, with Astaire and Judy Garland; and *Holiday Inn*, with Astaire, Crosby, Marjorie

Reynolds and Virginia Dale. This last film, of course, introduced the song "White Christmas" to the world; it won an Oscar for best song and would become the largest-selling song ever written.

It would be incorrect to imply that Berlin's career ended there, but the 1940s probably marked the pinnacle of his success. Still, the 1950s produced the films *Annie Get Your Gun*, *There's No Business Like Show Business*, and *White Christmas* (for which Berlin wrote "Count Your Blessings Instead of Sheep," among other songs.)

Of course, not all Berlin's songs were from the movies. He found time to pen other music, too, including the soulful "Suppertime" and the ultimate patriotic tribute, "God Bless America." In all, he composed over 1,500 songs. "And it is there we find our history, our holidays, our homes, and our hearts," Walter Cronkite was moved to remark on the songwriter's 100th birthday.

Irving Berlin died in 1989 at the age of 101.

Scandal

I'M STILL NOT SURE whether Bob Whelan knew when he made the assignment where it would lead me. Dr. Whelan was a political science professor at Georgia Institute of Technology in Atlanta, and a diehard college basketball fan. He was teaching a course on corruption in government, and when it came time to select a topic for our quarterly research papers, he asked me to do mine on the college basketball scandals that came to light in 1951.

"I think you'll find it interesting," I remember him saying, with a smile I later learned he reserved for gross understatements.

It turned out to be a fascinating assignment, and it led me right back to Sullivan County.

That's right, the darkest chapter in the history of college basketball—a point-shaving scandal that eventually would involve thirty-two players from seven colleges fixing eighty-six games in twenty-three cities in seventeen states—had its roots in Sullivan County. It is a part of county history most people would like to forget, but it is a part of county history nonetheless.

RETROSPECT

It was late February, 1951; the basketball team from the City College of New York was returning home on the train from Philadelphia where they had just trounced Temple University.

CCNY was being hailed throughout the nation as the greatest college basketball team of all time. The Lavender and Black had won both of college basketball's biggest year-end tournaments, the NCAA and the NIT, the year before—the only time that feat has ever been accomplished—and they were projected as favorites to capture both tournaments again.

But, as the train approached New Brunswick, New Jersey, a man summoned the team's coach, the legendary Nat Holman, to a private car. "I've got some bad news for you, coach," the man reportedly said. "I've got orders to pick up some of your boys."

The man was from the Manhattan district attorney's office, and before he and his colleagues were through, college basketball, Madison Square Garden, and the Sullivan County resort industry would all be dragged through the mud, and none of the three would ever be the same. The investigation eventually revealed that points were being shaved—that is, players were conspiring to win games by fewer points than their teams were favored by—in college basketball at least as far back as 1949. It hit the big-time in the summer of 1950, when a major gambler, Salvatore Sollazzo, and a former college player who had shaved points in the past, Eddie Gard, met at Grossinger's Hotel.

Gard, who would be a senior at Long Island University that fall, was playing on the Grossinger team in the informal Borscht Belt league, as were many of his LIU teammates, including Sherman White (the guard most experts considered the best player in the country), LeRoy Smith and Adolph Bigos. Connie Schaff and Jim Brasco of New York University, and Zeke Zawoluk of St. John's, also played for Grossinger's that summer. It was, as Stanley Cohen pointed out in his book on the scandals, *The Game They Played*, "a unit which probably could have beaten any college team in the country."

Klein's Hillside also had a powerhouse team that summer, led by CCNY star Ed Warner; so did Kutsher's, which always fielded a strong squad.

Competition in this Borscht league may have been informal, but it was always spirited, and, as it turned out, provided a fertile

ENTERTAINMENT

spawning ground for point shaving. "The Catskills needed no leagues, no standings, no champion," writes Stefan Kanfer in his study of the Catskill resort industry, *Summer World*. "They offered something more compelling: the wager... Bets were not made on the team, but on the number of points scored."

In order to make the games more interesting for the spectators, social directors might pass out numbers to spectators for a dollar a piece. The numbers represented the total number of points scored in that game. A player, or players, might conspire with a spectator to control the outcome and finish the game on a particular number, then split the winnings with the spectator who held that number.

This background was one on which Gard and Sollazzo decided they could capitalize in a big way. They traveled the circuit that summer, recruiting as many "name" players they could contact. It would be unfair to say that Gard and Sollazzo were responsible for *all* the college basketball games that were fixed as part of the massive point-shaving scandals that came to light later, but they were perhaps the biggest participants in the scheme.

Gard was a former college player of modest ability by the summer of 1950. Although he was to enter his senior year at Long Island University that fall, he had used up his three years of eligibility. He knew many of the best players in the country and had access to many others. Sollazzo was an ex-con, a jewelry manufacturer who couldn't resist a gamble, and liked a sure thing. The two were thrown together at Grossinger's, decided to collaborate on a scheme to fix games, and began contacting players they knew could control the outcome.

"Sollazzo seldom stayed in one place," Kanfer notes. "Customarily he and Gard traversed the mountain roads, scouting basketball teams for corruptible talent." Sherman White, playing at Grossinger's that summer, was an obvious choice. Gard introduced him to Sollazzo, and the fix was in. For $1,000 a game, White would help keep the score within the betting line. White got teammates Adolph Bigos and LeRoy Smith involved. Soon it was so big that it was virtually inevitable that it would be found out.

Eventually, gamblers trying to get in on a good thing contacted the wrong player. Manhattan College center Junius Kellogg reported a bribe offer to the Manhattan DA's office, and a trap was sprung on the gamblers. An investigation, which soon reached well into the nation's heartland, revealed that games were fixed in at least seventeen states in the late 1940s and early '50s.

It is inaccurate to blame the point-shaving schemes entirely on the atmosphere that existed at the Catskills' resorts, or on the college ballplayers who spent their summers working—and playing—there. But that the resort atmosphere played some role in the scandals is undeniable. So, when the whistle had been blown, the outcry was loud and clear. Many of the colleges involved were from New York. The Catskill resorts were the culprits, many said. Keep the ballplayers away.

Among those to yell loudest was Kansas Coach Phog Allen, a basketball institution. "In the East, the boys, particularly those who participate in the resort hotel leagues during the summer months, are thrown into an environment which cannot help but breed the evil which more and more is coming to light," Allen pontificated.

Later, it was revealed that Bradley University, in Peoria, Illinois, was among the most active of the point-shaving teams, and had, in fact, thrown a game to Allen's Jayhawks the year before. Nonetheless, Nat Holman of CCNY, a man who had regularly placed many of his better players on summer hotel teams, agreed with Allen. Calling the hotel teams "schools of crime," Holman forbid his players to play in the Catskills.

So, shortly after it had reached its heyday in the late 1940s, the Borscht basketball circuit was discontinued in 1951. Summers in the Catskills would never be the same. Kanfer quotes a "Catskill veteran" in *A Summer World*: "After the scandals, the gyms were quiet. The big sport was 'Simon Says.' For entertainment we went back to singers and dancers and stand-up comics."

This put a serious crimp in the entertainment plans of major hotels. Managing directors found it nearly impossible to find a pastime to replace basketball, and in the spring of 1953, the owner of the Flagler Hotel in South Fallsburg decided to do something about it: Jack Barsky's plan involved not the amateur talent of top-flight colleges, but the more mature professional players of the National Basketball Association, players like George Mikan, Bob Cousy, Paul Arizin, Neil Johnston, and Ed MacCauley. Barsky's plan did not include individual hotel teams, but suggested that two teams made up of NBA stars tour the Catskills for a series of night exhibition games.

Barsky wrote to NBA Commissioner Maurice Podoloff and asked him to allow the professional players to moonlight in the Catskills for the summer. The NBA was in its infancy in 1953, and it needed all the exposure it could muster. Professional basketball, in fact, although growing in stature by the early '50s, had yet to supplant the college game as the fans' favorite. So Barsky's proposal must have seemed tempting to Podoloff.

The Liberty *Register* reported Barsky's plan promised that "no hotel guest would be charged admission," but that a flat guarantee would be arranged for the players and the league to divide up. "Barsky, who has both indoor and outdoor courts at the Flagler, said he would be willing to hold the first basketball game as a trial and predicted other hotels would soon ask for games," the *Register* reported.

Barsky wrote, "Basketball was always one of the most popular sports in the Catskill resort area, and a program of professional games throughout the summer would be a tremendous boom to the sport. There are upwards of two million potential customers in the Catskill area and those that are exposed to professional basketball for the first time would become steady customers when league play begins."

Despite the obvious appeal of this proposal and pleas from other hotel owners in the area who felt the arrangement could benefit both Sullivan County and the league, the NBA refused to change its rules, and the plan to form a summer barnstorming circuit never materialized.

Of course, just a few years later, some of the NBA's top players would make regular trips to the mountains each year to take part in an annual game to benefit Cincinnati Royals star Maurice Stokes, who was stricken by encephalitis.

As big as the Maurice Stokes game would become over the years, however, it would never eclipse the memories of the great rivalries of the old Borscht circuit, when some of the best players in the land called Sullivan County their summer home.

RETROSPECT

Sonny Liston

THERE ARE TWO THINGS I will never forget about the first time I saw Charles "Sonny" Liston on a South Fallsburg street: the scowl he always seemed to wear, and the size of his hands.

Both features were integral to his rise to the top of the world's heavyweight boxing heap in the early 1960s, a rise that culminated in his two-punch knockout of Floyd Patterson in September 1962, in a bout for which he prepared at the Pines Hotel.

There was a time when Liston was just about the most feared man in the world. He had already been arrested nineteen times before he fought the popular Patterson for the heavyweight crown, and his troubles with the law did not end with that dramatic first-round victory.

His perpetual scowl notwithstanding, the Liston who spent time in the Sullivan County Catskills, prepping for a championship fight that lasted only a bit over a minute, was not the brooding troublemaker cops in cities from Philadelphia to St. Louis swore he was. In Sullivan County, Liston was quiet and serious, and a church goer. He was so popular with the parish priest in Woodbourne that the Sunday before Liston's first fight with Cassius Clay in 1964, the priest implored an altar boy to light a candle for the young man from Louisville. "Let's hope Charles doesn't kill him," he said.

Locals who spent time with Liston also remember him fondly. "The scowl was just a front, an act," says Morris Gold of South Fallsburg, who knew Liston even before he came to the Pines to train. "Sonny Liston was the gentlest man you'd ever want to meet. He was good with kids, and he loved to laugh. Unfortunately, people never gave him a chance. Many just assumed he was as mean as he looked."

But a scowl alone, no matter how well practiced, does not win boxing matches, let alone championships. As a fighter, Liston had considerably more going for him: mammoth hands (his fists measured fifteen inches around), for example.

"His hands were so large, I couldn't believe it," the Reverend Alois Stevens, a Catholic priest who was instrumental in getting Liston started in boxing at the Missouri State Penitentiary, once told *Sports Illustrated* magazine. "They always had trouble with his gloves, trouble getting them on when his hands were wrapped," he said. "He was the most perfect specimen of manhood I had ever seen. Powerful arms, big shoulders. Pretty soon he was knocking out everyone in the gym."

In fact, Liston was so powerful he could knock out an opponent with his jab. No less an authority than Patterson rated him the hardest-hitting heavyweight of his time. And Liston's powerful physique made him virtually unforgettable. "He was massive," remembers Daniel Ingber of South Fallsburg, who was seven years old when he used to see Liston run past his house. "My most vivid memory of him is putting my brother Mark, who was sick at the time and died a short time later, on his shoulders and running up the hill like that."

His title-winning victory over Patterson, for which he trained at the Pines, and his subsequent defense of that title in a brief rematch, were the highlights of Liston's career. Life was all downhill for Sonny after that. He surrendered the crown in a controversial seven-round loss to Clay, and then lost again to the same man, now named Muhammad Ali, in an infamous bout many observers claim was fixed.

Four fights—the two with Patterson which placed him at the top of the world, and the two with Ali which made him the butt of vicious barroom jokes—effectively defined Liston's boxing career, and perhaps his sullied life, as well. Even his death, under questionable circumstances in Las Vegas in December 1970, could not bring him peace.

Boxing and the Catskills

THE ENDURING MARRIAGE of top-notch boxers and Sullivan County all started in 1934, when Barney Ross came to Grossinger's to train. He couldn't have known that he was in the vanguard of what was to become an integral part of Sullivan County history. Boxing and the Catskills would be inseparable forever after.

Over the next few decades, professional boxers of all weight classifications—champions and also-rans alike—flocked to Sullivan County resorts to train for important bouts. It was a symbiotic relationship made in heaven—the resorts furnished the boxers state-of-the-art training facilities; the boxers, in turn, generated considerable publicity for the resorts.

That's exactly what Milton Blackstone had in mind when he lured Barney Ross to Grossinger's.

Ross, one of a handful of successful Jewish prizefighters, was the lightweight champion of the world, and was preparing to take on Jimmy McLarnin for the welterweight crown. He was easily sold on the idea of training at the Big G.

The hotel, on the other hand, wasn't so sure that a pugilist, even a world champion, would project the proper image for the resort. Malke Grossinger, especially, balked at the notion. "What is this Ross, a drinker, that he must do such a thing?" she reportedly said. "He can't hold a steady job?"

But Ross came, nonetheless. Still, Malke was unconvinced; she refused to greet him upon his arrival or to watch him train. Then one day she inadvertently bumped into Ross in the hotel kitchen. "This is the box-fighter?" she asked. "He was Friday night in the synagogue." A Catskill tradition had begun.

Ingemar Johansson. He trained for championship fights at Grossinger's. (Photo courtesy Lou Goldstein)

Dozens of sportswriters followed Ross to Liberty, and over the next few weeks they filed daily stories from the hotel. There wasn't a boxing fan anywhere who didn't eventually know about Grossinger's.

It is perhaps fitting that Ross—an Orthodox Jew who adhered to a kosher diet—started the trend of boxers training at Catskill resorts. But it wasn't long before a diverse list of fighters followed him, and, although Grossinger's had gotten a head start on the rest of the county's resorts, other major hotels soon got into the act as well. When Rocky Marciano trained at Grossinger's for a bout with Ezzard Charles, Charles trained at Kutsher's. Both hotels benefited from the exposure, which included live interviews from the resorts on Edward R. Murrow's television news show.

ENTERTAINMENT

Still, Grossinger's hosted more fighters than did any other Catskill hotel. Lew Jenkins, Max Baer, Billy Conn, Joey Maxim, Randy Turpin, Gene Fullmer, Ingemar Johansson, Joey Archer, Nino Benvenuti, Ken Buchanan, Jerry Quarry, Ken Norton, Larry Holmes, Michael Spinks, Roberto Duran, and Evander Holyfield, among others, would eventually train there.

Sonny Liston trained at the Pines in 1962 for his heavyweight championship fight with Floyd Patterson. Emile Griffith, world welterweight and middleweight titleholder, trained at the Concord, as did Gerry Cooney and a host of others—including Muhammad Ali, arguably the greatest heavyweight of all time and the only man to hold the heavyweight title three times.

These fighters were just names on the marquis to some fans, but to many others the intimate nature of the Sullivan County hotels provided a unique opportunity to get to know the fighters. Lou Goldstein, who spent decades in the resort life, has rubbed elbows with as many boxers as anyone. He was instrumental in bringing some of boxing's most colorful characters to the Catskills, and has vivid memories of some of them.

Rocky Marciano. The undefeated champion trained at Grossinger's and later lived at the hotel. (Photo courtesy Lou Goldstein)

Known to millions around the world today as 'Mr. Simon Says,' Goldstein was the sports director at Grossinger's during the hotel's heyday as a haven for top-notch fighters. "I made a show out of their training," he says. "Every day at 2:30, they'd be sparring. I'd precede that with a detailed explanation of the fighter's techniques, his equipment, his training regimen, every facet of his routine. Then I'd interview the fighter for the guests afterwards, and take their questions. For all this we'd charge a dollar a head, and we always had a few hundred spectators. Nobody else did it like that."

Goldstein met hundreds of boxers at Grossinger's during his tenure there, and became close personal friends with many of them. He can rattle off dozens of champions he worked with, including some of the greatest fighters of all time. But it isn't just the champions he remembers. "We had some of boxing's most colorful characters at the hotel," he says. "Men like Joey Archer, who fought Emile Griffith twice for the middleweight title in the 1960s, losing close bouts each time. Archer was always the sharpest dresser at the hotel. I always called him the Irish Gentleman.

"The most entertaining of all the fighters was Roberto Duran. He was always great, a very funny man. He spoke little English, except if it had to do with money. That he understood. Duran was a marvelous dancer, and always put on a show. And he'd spend hours patiently signing autographs for the guests."

Goldstein found Dick Tiger, who held both the middleweight and light-heavyweight crowns at different times in the 1960s, the most gentlemanly of all the fighters who came to the hotel, "especially with the ladies," he says. "Jerry Quarry was another gentleman," Goldstein says of the perennial contender of the '60s and '70s. "He trained here for his fight with Joe Frazier, which, by the way, was the most devastating six rounds of boxing I ever saw. Quarry could really take a punch, but cut easily."

When it came to taking a punch, though, one man stands out in Goldstein's mind. "No one could take a punch like Oscar Bonavena," he says of the Argentine Bull. "He was very strong, and didn't cut, either. You just couldn't knock him out."

Some fighters were natural showmen, easy to work with and fun to watch during training. Goldstein places lightweight champions Kenny Buchanan and Ray "Boom-Boom" Mancini, and heavyweight champs Ken Norton and Larry Holmes in this category. "I remember when Norton was training here for a bout with Ali, who was over at the Concord," he says. "Ali would show up here while Kenny was sparring and annoy him. We'd have all we could do to keep Kenny from chasing him. Holmes was beautiful to watch. He was always imitating Ali. Buchanan was interesting to watch, too, and Mancini was a great interview."

Other fighters provided different memories: Michael Spinks ran the most professional training camp; Livingstone Bramble kept snakes in his room (a fact one chambermaid found out the hard way); Ingemar Johansson paraded a string of women in and out of his. ("He broke four beds during one stay," Goldstein remembers.)

ENTERTAINMENT

But of all the fighters who called Grossinger's their temporary home, one stands out above all the rest.

Rocky Marciano, born Rocco Francis Marchegiano, originally hailed from Brockton, Massachusetts, but Liberty—as in Grossinger's—was his adopted home. Many fighters came to the mountains for a few weeks to train for a fight, but Marciano came to stay.

"He lived at the airport for years," says Goldstein. "We set up a training camp for him there, and eventually it became his home as well. In fact, he wore 'Grossinger's, N.Y.' on the back of his robe when he fought. At first, they didn't want to let him do that—the boxing officials. Fighters couldn't advertise resorts on their robes, but I explained to John Condon, who was head of boxing promotion for Madison Square Garden, that Grossinger's was not just a resort, it was Rocky's home. Grossinger's was an official post office, you know. So they allowed it. It was great publicity for the hotel."

And the Big G couldn't have found a better standard bearer than Marciano, who never lost a professional fight. "He was incredible, there was no one like Rocky," Goldstein declares. "He could really take a punch, absorb a lot of punishment, and he used to beat an opponent on the arms and to the body. He would relentlessly attack the body, and soon the guy's legs would give out."

Marciano's determination became almost as legendary as his punching power. Occasionally, on the brink of defeat, it appeared that he simply refused to be beaten. "I remember one particular time—the second Ezzard Charles fight in 1954," Goldstein says. "Marciano was cut badly. His nose was actually ripped from his face. The ring doctor took one look at him and wanted to stop the fight. Rocky told him he needed just one more round. 'Just give me one more,' he says, 'then you can stop it.' In that last round he knocked Charles out. It was as if he knew he had to do it and he did it."

Marciano made his way through the entire heavyweight division, taking on all comers without a setback—claims by critics that his managers ducked certain fighters they felt could beat Rocky notwithstanding—and retired undefeated in 1956. And, unlike so many other fighters, he remained retired. He also remained in Sullivan County, and became a common site in the area, often in the company of Morris Gold of South Fallsburg. "I was Rocky's bodyguard," Gold says of the man with whom he became a close friend.

Rocky also had a reputation for being somewhat stingy. "I used to call him the man with the short arms and the deep pockets," Goldstein says.

But one local resident remembers Marciano most for a possession with which he parted. "I repaired some damage to his Cadillac once," former body shop owner Yits Kantrowitz of Woodridge says. "And he shows up to pick up the car with a pair of his boxing trunks for me. I'll never part with them, and I'll never forget Rocky Marciano."

Rocky Marciano, Sullivan County's adopted son, and the only man in boxing history to retire as undefeated heavyweight champion, died in a plane crash in 1969.

Chapter Six

Crime and Punishment

Edward C. Dollard: Hero Cop

THE DATE—Sept. 6, 1923—is indelibly etched in Edward J. Dollard's mind. That's the night his father, Edward C. Dollard, a village of Monticello police officer, interrupted three Weehauken, New Jersey men as they burglarized a Broadway auto parts store, and was shot and killed attempting to arrest them.

Dollard left Monticello in 1939, eventually settling in Queensbury, near Glens Falls. He was thirteen at the time of his father's death, the oldest of four children. His memory of that distant night is vivid; his recollection of the fateful events flawless, despite the passage of time.

"As young as I was, I can never forget any detail of what happened," he said. "Dad was born in Hoboken, and had been a Pinkerton detective before moving to Monticello, where he joined the police force. There were only two or three cops on the force back then, except during the summer months, when they might have had eight or ten, and they alternated from year to year as chief. Dad was chief at the time, and he was in civilian clothes the night it happened.

"He was on his way home, walking up Broadway, when he came across another officer, Al Conroy, who was on duty at the time, eating his dinner in one of the restaurants. So dad stopped to talk. Conroy said that he had to go check in at the Oakley Avenue call box, just up the street. Dad told him to finish his dinner, that he was going right by there, and he'd ring in for him. He got to Oakley Avenue and was ringing in when he spotted these two men loading auto parts and tires from the rear of a Broadway store into their car. He cornered them, and got them up against the car, not realizing that there was another one of them. The third guy came up behind him and shot him three times in the back."

Mortally wounded, Dollard's father was able to call out, alerting Conroy, and the burglars-turned-murderers were captured a short time later. Meanwhile, village officials were faced with the prospect of informing Dollard's family of his death.

"Two men—John Cooke and a man named Mapes—came to the house around two or three o'clock in the morning, they woke us up," Dollard told me. And then he paused, obviously struggling with the painful memory. "My mother knew right away what it was. I don't know how, but she did. 'It's Ed, isn't it?' she asked them. 'He's dead, isn't he?'"

As news of the shooting spread, some of the townspeople organized a lynch mob, so the three men were kept under heavy guard until a trial date could be set. Dollard said that an underground tunnel connecting the jail to the courthouse was used to transport the prisoners back and forth between the buildings.

Two of the men were eventually tried and convicted—one was sentenced to the electric chair, although his sentence was later commuted—but the third one escaped, despite all the precautions. "He was never recaptured," Dollard said. "Although I came within minutes of catching up to him once myself."

Dollard spent a year and a half as a Monticello cop, then joined the Erie Railroad as a detective. Ironically, one of his earliest assignments placed him in Weehauken. "I made it my business to try to find the guy," he said, referring to the murderer who had escaped. "I trailed him for months. One night I stopped by a tavern where I knew he hung out, and the bartender told me he had left just minutes before. I tried to follow him, but I couldn't pick up his trail. Now I thank God that I didn't catch him, because I was young then, and I would have plugged him for sure. I know I wanted to. I thank God everyday I didn't."

CRIME AND PUNISHMENT

Gangland Killing Led to Courtroom Dramatics

More than fifty years ago, a Sullivan County grand jury indicted several men in the gangland murder of Walter Sage. Some of the most dramatic trials ever to take place in Sullivan County court followed.

The trials revealed that Sage, a Brooklyn gangster with a considerable police record, had been lured to the Hotel Evans in Loch Sheldrake and stabbed thirty-seven times with an ice pick. His body was weighted down with a thirty-pound rock and the frame from a slot machine and thrown into Swan Lake. However, buoyed by gasses generated by decomposition, the body eventually floated to the surface of the quiet lake, where it was discovered on July 31, 1937.

The ensuing investigation into the murder took nearly three years, and it wasn't until May 1940 that indictments were finally handed up. One of the first to be indicted in Sage's murder was Hollywood film extra Irving "Big Gangi" Cohen, alias Jack Gordon. Following the indictment, Sullivan County District Attorney William Deckelman and Sheriff Harry Borden traveled to the west coast, where Cohen had been picked up and was being held on a fugitive warrant by authorities in Los Angeles.

Swan Lake. This tranquil scene belies the excitement that followed the discovery of slot machine overseer Walter Sage's body floating in the lake on July 31, 1937. The Stevensensville Hotel is in the background to the right and the President Hotel can be seen far left. (Author's collection)

The trip to the Golden State was just one of many jaunts for Deckelman in connection with the Sage murder. He had already spent considerable time in Manhattan, tracking down and interviewing Cohen's cohorts, two of whom—Anthony "Dukie" Maffatore and Abraham "Pretty" Levine—had implicated Cohen in Sage's death.

Sage, it was discovered, had led far from an angelic

life. He had an extensive police record in New York City, had been questioned in the 1932 murder of Israel Goldberg on a Brownsville street corner, and had been arrested in 1933 in connection with the murder of Brooklyn gangster Alex Alpert. Why gang members turned against him, however, was never made clear.

Deckelman was an able prosecutor and had built an enviable record as county district attorney, but he had his hands full in the Cohen trial. Sullivan County Court Judge George L. Cooke had appointed Liberty attorney Albert Decker to assist Deckelman, since there were, at that time, no full-time assistant district attorneys, and Deckelman needed all the help he could get. There were dozens of leads to follow, cleverly conceived alibis to discredit, and three-year-old clues to investigate. Many of the prosecution's witnesses were untrustworthy, to say the least; some sported considerable police records of their own.

Cohen was defended by Saul Price and Moses Kove, and although Deckelman appeared to present a strong case throughout the trial, Cohen was acquitted amidst an incredible flood of publicity.

It wasn't until December 1943 that another well-known gangster, Jack Drucker, was apprehended in connection with the Sage murder. Drucker was subsequently tried and convicted, and in May 1944 was sentenced by Judge Cooke to twenty-five years to life for the crime.

Walter Sage may have been one the most well-publicized of the murder victims discovered in Sullivan County during that time—few who have ever seen the picture of his body, beaten and bloody, his feet neatly bound with rope and tied to the iron frame of the slot machine, will ever forget it—but he certainly wasn't the only one. Indeed, the exploits of Murder, Incorporated, were much more far-reaching.

A body was discovered floating on the surface of Loch Sheldrake in 1939; a subsequent investigation showed the man, identified as Maurice "Frenchy" Carillot, a reputed drug dealer, had been shot five times and stabbed seven. Another man was found in a lime pit in a barn near Hurleyville. There were, no doubt, others.

Most people today are unaware that the tentacles of organized crime once had a firm grip on the region; virtually every part of the county was touched in some way. The resorts of the Fallsburg, Thompson and Liberty areas were, as one might expect, the focus of

CRIME AND PUNISHMENT

most of the syndicate's activities: Slot machines and gaming rooms could be found in many of the hotels. Bootleg liquor was present throughout the county, and moonshine distilleries were broken up in a number of out-of-the-way places.

"There was a certain atmosphere throughout the county then," one old-timer who grew up in South Fallsburg told me. "It was generally known that slot machines were in many of the hotels, and the feeling among many working-class people in this area was that political corruption, even on the county level, allowed much of this activity to occur unimpeded."

White Lake was a hotbed of criminal activity, so much so that its unsavory reputation led North White Lake to adopt a new name—Kauneonga Lake—so it wouldn't be so closely identified with its neighbor to the south. Other lakes in various parts of the county, notably Swan Lake and Loch Sheldrake, were rumored to be popular burial grounds for the New York City gangs.

But Judge Cooke was one official not given to allowing the unimpeded breaking of the law. "My father was a seasoned magistrate, and wasn't fazed by the Murder, Incorporated, trials," says Lawrence H. Cooke, former chief judge of the New York State Court of Appeals. "Murder was nothing new to him. Although I wasn't involved to any extent in the trials, I do remember them well. In fact, one of the defense attorneys told me many years later that my father had presided over the court in wonderful fashion. The court transcripts revealed a perfect court record, leaving the defense attorney no chance for a reversal.

"He had been the district attorney for six years, and had prosecuted murderers. He was a fine trial lawyer before he was a judge, so he wasn't uncomfortable with the seriousness of what was before him."

William Deckelman was the county's district attorney during much of the Murder, Incorporated, activity. Deckelman spent years meticulously investigating the murders the syndicate was believed responsible for in Sullivan County, and he vigorously prosecuted Gangi Cohen for the murder of Walter Sage.

Nancy McKeen of Jeffersonville, Deckelman's granddaughter, was often told of the tension the investigation and trial placed on her family. "I can remember hearing that certain threats were made against my grandfather, and against his family," she says. "Of course, he would never speak of them in front of us, but I am told sometimes things were tense."

Edith Paul of Jeffersonville has similar memories. Her father, Dr. Cameron Gain, was county coroner during a good portion of the murder investigations. "I can remember one night, it was fairly late, someone came to the front door and told my father that they needed him in Hurleyville, that they had just found a body in a lime pit there," she said. "During that time period, it seemed every time someone came to the door or whenever the phone would ring at night, we'd all have a certain feeling, and wonder—what is it going to be this time?"

Drucker Trial Opened Syndicate Can of Worms

THE DETAILS were unavailable, and in fact were probably unnecessary; the newspaper headline told the entire story.

"Jack Drucker Arrested in Delaware By FBI," read the front page of the Dec. 28, 1943, edition of the *Sullivan County Evening News*. "Murder, Inc. Gunman Will Face Trial For Killing in Sullivan," the subhead continued.

Jacob "Jack" Drucker's arrest was a long time coming. The former Hurleyville farm boy had been implicated in the ice-pick murder of Brooklyn gangster Walter Sage, whose trussed-up body was pulled from Swan Lake on July 31, 1937. A lengthy investigation followed, which took Sullivan County District Attorney William Deckelman, the Sullivan County Sheriff's Department, and the New York State Police from one end of the United States to the other in search of clues. Drucker was finally indicted with several others in 1940.

By the time of Drucker's arrest, Deckelman had stepped down as district attorney and had been replaced by the newly-elected Benjamin Newberg. For Newberg, the arrest couldn't have come at a worse time. "Ben had just been elected in November," his widow, Barbara Newberg of South Fallsburg remembers. "He wasn't even sworn in yet when Drucker was arrested. Right away he had to prepare for the trial."

Drucker's trial was the second in the Sage case. Film extra Gangi Cohen had been tried and acquitted in 1940, despite a vigorous and thorough prosecution by Deckelman. The feeling was that the witnesses who took the stand against Cohen, many of whom were known gangsters themselves, were less than credible.

Word was that if Newberg was unsuccessful in his prosecution of Drucker for the Sage murder, he was prepared to proceed with cases against him in four other murders in the county: Charles "Chink" Sherman in 1935; Irving Ashkenaz in 1936; Maurice "Frenchy" Carillot in 1938; and Hyman Yuran in 1940. As it was, these trials were unnecessary; the jury found Drucker guilty of murdering Sage. Star witness for the prosecution was confessed murderer Albert "Allie" Tannenbaum (who spent most of his childhood years in Rock Hill, and later Loch Sheldrake), who told the court that he had discussed the murder with Drucker and that Drucker had told him he had killed Sage under orders from gang leader "Pittsburgh" Phil Strauss.

State police and other officials gather around a barn on the Drucker farm near Hurleyville where the body of Chink Sherman was found on election eve, 1935. Drucker eluded police until 1944. (Author's collection)

The jury deliberated for about five hours before finding Drucker guilty, and he was later sentenced to twenty-five years to life in prison by County Judge George L. Cooke. Drucker died in prison.

"My husband knew that Albert Tannenbaum would be a key witness," Mrs. Newberg says. "The first thing he did when he realized he was going to have to try the case was to pick him up in Florida. Tannenbaum was very frightened. While he was here, he was kept in protective custody. Not even I knew where he was being kept.

"This had always been a wide open county," she continues, "with slot machines in the hotels, and big-time gamblers doing regular business in some of them. I'm not saying my husband single-handedly cleaned it up, but I think he had a big part. I know we both spent many a sleepless night because of the job he was doing."

When the Drucker trial was over, Newberg issued a statement that made it clear that the reign of Murder, Incorporated, in Sullivan County had ended. "All of the killers in whom we were interested are either in jail or dead," he told one of the county's weekly newspapers, the *Bulletin-Sentinel*, believing the book on a dark chapter in the county's history was closed.

And so most people thought it had been. But there it is, in black and white, in Carl Sifakis' well-researched compendium, *The Mafia Encyclopedia*: the confession of another man for the crime for which Drucker was convicted.

Sifakis is a highly respected crime reporter and freelance writer who has written several books, including *The Encyclopedia of American Crime* and *The Catalog of Crime*, so it is hard to argue with his contention that renowned hit man Pittsburgh Phil Strauss actually had murdered Sage.

"Phil always said he could learn more about murder," Sifakis wrote about organized crime's top killer. "When he executed Walter Sage, a New York mobster who was knocking down on the syndicate's slot machine profits, he lashed Sage's body to a pinball machine after ice-picking him thirty-two times, and then dumped him in a Catskills lake. Seven days later, the grisly package floated to the surface, due to the buoyancy caused by gases in the decomposing body. 'How about that,' Phil observed sagely, 'With this bum, you gotta be a doctor or he floats.'"

Drucker had insisted all along that Strauss was the murderer, but he had no alibi for the night of the slaying, and everyone who knows anything about syndicate hit men know they always have alibis when they fulfill a contract.

Could the wrong man have been convicted of the murder?

Sifakis worked on an old manual typewriter, badly in need of a new ribbon, and jotted down almost illegible notes in pencil. But he knew his stuff. "No contradiction here at all," he told me emphatically when presented with the history of the Sage murder. "The kill team was headed by Pittsburgh Phil and included, among others, Gangi Cohen and Jack Drucker, and Pretty Levine."

CRIME AND PUNISHMENT

Pretty Levine had been one of the primary witnesses, along with Dukie Maffatore, against Cohen in the first murder trial. They had saved themselves by turning state's evidence, but if Pittsburgh Phil had really been part of the execution squad, as Sifakis claimed, and had been implicated by one or more of his accomplices, why was he never tried for the crime, as well—especially since Drucker's defense was that Strauss had killed Sage?

"Phil was implicated in dozens of killings, and went to the chair for another one," Sifakis maintains. "Drucker's defense that Phil had done it had no legal meaning, since, as an accomplice, he was equally guilty. And besides, he was ID'ed as the one holding the bloody ice pick."

So, in all probability, Drucker, Cohen, Strauss, Levine and Maffatore were all guilty of the Sage killing, just as District Attorney William Deckelman, who tried the Cohen case, had originally maintained. Which one had actually wielded the murder weapon was, legally speaking, insignificant.

What is indisputable is that Sullivan County is forever linked with the most notorious and prolific of Murder, Incorporated's professional killers: Pittsburgh Phil Strauss, a man believed to have been responsible for more than 100 murders. Strauss was finally executed for one of them on June 12, 1941.

Though some of the crime syndicate's local activities came to light during the Sage trials—including the snuffing of Chink Sherman, Irving Ashkenaz, Frenchy Carillot and Hyman Yuran—there were apparently other rubouts in the county which received very little media attention.

Take, for instance, the case of Sol Goldstein, better known to his mob friends as Jack. He was honeymooning at a secluded cottage in Glen Wild during the summer of 1936 when his number was called by a mob big shot. (Though Goldstein had decided to cut his ties with the Brooklyn-based gangs with which he had run since boyhood, he apparently knew too much about the activities of his associates.) A contract was put out on him, and Pittsburgh Phil Strauss was commissioned to make the hit. Pretty Levine and Dukey Maffatore—two young mobsters who later turned state's evidence and provided authorities with the details of this and dozens of other crimes—were

141

dispatched from Brooklyn to Loch Sheldrake, where Strauss often stayed at the Hotel Evans, to help out.

Strauss knew Goldstein had to be separated from his new wife before he could be hit, but Goldstein knew Phil, so he would have suspected something was up had he been approached by Strauss. However, he wasn't acquainted with Levine or Maffatore, nor with Pittsburgh Phil's two other henchmen, Mikey Syckoff and Jack Cutler. Goldstein's bride remembered later that Jack received a telephone call as he was dressing for dinner one night, and a few minutes later was picked up by a car with three men in it (she didn't know them, though they were later identified as Levine, Syckoff, and Cutler).

Levine provided authorities with the remaining details: One of the young trio almost immediately wrapped his arm around Goldstein's throat (or "mugged" him, in mob parlance) and Levine slugged him with a hammer, just hard enough to knock him out. They had been given explicit orders by Strauss not to kill Jack—Pittsburgh Phil, who had an old score to settle with Goldstein, wanted to make the hit himself.

Goldstein was transported to Loch Sheldrake, where Strauss wrapped his unconscious form in a blanket and trussed it with rope. Then, with Allie Tannenbaum and Jack Drucker (who would later help him with the Walter Sage murder), Pittsburgh Phil rowed to the middle of Loch Sheldrake and personally dumped the bundle overboard.

Strauss was given the double pleasure of fulfilling a contract and settling an old score at the same time. And he was more fortunate with the dumping of this body than he would be the following summer with Sage's (Goldstein's body has apparently never surfaced), and the lack of a *corpus delecti* prevented authorities from ever prosecuting the members of the kill team for Goldstein's murder.

There were at least four other mob hits linked to Sullivan by law enforcement officials during the 1940 probes of Murder, Incorporated, including the rub out of Chink Sherman, whose body was found in a lime pit on Jack Drucker's farm near Hurleyville in 1936.

Sherman was a strong-arm for Waxey Gordon and a narcotics dealer known throughout the underworld as the "Chinaman," or simply "Chink." Like Gordon, he was Dutch Schultz's bitter enemy.

CRIME AND PUNISHMENT

While Schultz lingered dying in a hospital bed following his shooting in the men's room of a Newark chophouse, he deliriously babbled orders to imaginary underlings—copiously recorded by a police stenographer and eventually reprinted by the media. One of his last commands was, "Please crack down on the Chinaman's friends." A few weeks later, Sherman's body was uncovered.

Irving Ashkenaz was a taxicab owner in Manhattan who, in 1936, had been filling in special prosecutor Thomas E. Dewey on the mob's racketeering activities in that enterprise. Ashkenaz apparently got a bit carried away with his role as expert witness, and had come to Sullivan County to do some further investigations on his own. His body was found near the entrance to the Paramount Manor resort, draped across the running board of his cab, his feet still in the car, his face partially buried in the dirt of the road. Over the body, a sign hung. It read: Hotel of Happiness. Pittsburgh Phil Strauss, Allie Tannenbaum, and Gangy Cohen were eventually indicted in Ashkenaz's murder. The three were implicated in this and other crimes through the squealing of Abe "Kid Twist" Reles, Pretty Levine, and Dukey Maffatore.

Hyman Yuran, "a dress manufacturer of some affluence," was the man mainly responsible for breaking up Murder, Incorporated, according to Brooklyn prosecutor Burton Turkus. Lepke Buchalter, the industrial extortionist and one of the crime syndicate's top bosses—FBI Director J. Edgar Hoover once called him "the most dangerous criminal in the United States"—had infiltrated the garment industry by using Yuran's influence. When Lepke went on trial in 1939, Yuran was expected to be a key witness against him. That made him a marked man; Lepke had not reached the lofty heights of organized crime by allowing witnesses to testify against him.

Yuran was vacationing in Sullivan County in August 1939 when Lepke decided he should be hit. Pittsburgh Phil Strauss was dispatched to do the job. Strauss, from his base of operations at a Fallsburg hotel, enlisted the aid of Sholem Bernstein, Allie Tannenbaum, and Jack Drucker. Bernstein later told authorities that Strauss and Tannenbaum had knocked off Yuran, and he and Drucker helped bury the body. Bernstein said he had met Drucker in Fallsburg and had gone for a drive with him. Meanwhile, Yuran was heisted from a hotel night club and taken for a ride in his own car. By the time

Strauss and Tannenbaum—in Yuran's car—met Bernstein and Drucker, Yuran had been killed.

A grave site was chosen nearby, but it was quickly abandoned because the ground was so rocky; Strauss decided to bury the body in a lime-lined pit near the Rosemont Lodge swimming pool instead. Bernstein was directed to dispose of Yuran's car by driving it back to Brooklyn. Yuran's body was discovered early in 1940.

As unlikely as it might seem, whenever mob henchmen socialized in Sullivan County—despite the fact that they seemed to be constantly leaving bodies in their wake—they behaved as perfect gentlemen. That's exactly what made the new syndicate, formed in 1931, so dangerous: Its members were as much businessmen as they were killers. To be sure, there are those who still remember when many of these dreaded gangsters cavorted around the county as if they had not a care in the world. Few people here in the mountains—or elsewhere, for that matter—knew at the time just how despicable these people were.

So perhaps it is not surprising that, for the most part, the professional murderers who stayed in Sullivan County are remembered as gentlemen, classy free-spenders little different from many of the other guests who frequented the area's resorts. Except that they happened to kill people for a living and thrived on it.

Cy Plotkin's recollections are fairly typical. Plotkin's family owned the Woodlawn Villa, a hotel on White Lake which, for a time, was a favorite hangout for some of the killers. "I remember them well," Plotkin told me. "Several of them—Pittsburgh Phil, Abie Reles, Pretty Levine—spent considerable time at the hotel during 1934 and 1935. They never caused any trouble. They were always perfect gentlemen when they were there."

Before his good friend and co-worker Reles turned stool-pigeon, Pittsburgh Phil Strauss spent very little time behind bars. Strauss came to Woodlawn Villa after one such stay. "He must have just gotten out of jail," Plotkin recalled, "because his head was completely shaven. This was very unusual for Pittsburgh Phil, because he was always well-groomed and dressed just so." Indeed, the vain Strauss liked to think of himself as irresistible to women, the Beau Brummel of the gangster set.

For the most part, where these demons went, trouble usually followed, but Plotkin remembers only one occasion when the murderers were at the center of an altercation at his family's hotel: "It was one Labor Day weekend. There was a fight in the dining room, and they were throwing bottles at each other. My mother, though, was a pretty tough lady, and she put an end to that rather quickly. There was never any other trouble that I recall."

Reles's testimony put many of the mob's killers—including Pittsburgh Phil—on death row before he was permanently silenced by a fall from a fifth floor window while in police custody at the Half-Moon Hotel in Coney Island.

Most current Sullivan County residents have no memory—or only vague recollections—of the days when brazen murderers freely roamed the region, often leaving bodies in their wake. But those days really did exist, and will forever remain a part of the county's history.

Mobster May Have Thrown Away Millions

THE OLD PLAZA HOTEL in South Fallsburg is remembered for many things, including the fact that it was purported to be the first hotel in the Catskills with an elevator. It is also recalled for the slot machines that regularly entertained its guests during the 1930s, and for the fact that it was the favorite Catskill hangout of Jacob Shapiro.

Shapiro was better known to his mobster friends as "Gurrah." The nickname grew out of Shapiro's favorite expression—"get outta here"—which, when uttered through the gangster's clenched teeth sounded more like "gurrah da here."

Shapiro was introduced to the Plaza by his good friend and business associate Lepke Buchalter, and he used to bring his mother there to escape the summer heat of the city. In fact, his mother became a virtual fixture at the place. In his history of the Sullivan County resort industry, *A Summer World*, Stefan Kanfer quotes comedian Joey Adams recalling that Mrs. Shapiro was the "Queen Bee" of the hotel. "Everybody catered to her," Adams said. "Her son lined her path with gold. She was a lovely woman but only aware that her son must be a big man because everyone was so nice to her and she got everything she wanted."

Shapiro *was* a big man. He was the brawn to Buchalter's brains in the labor racketeering and extortion empire the latter built during the early days of the syndicate. But the ruins of the Plaza are still a reminder of a rare move Shapiro made without his diminutive partner in crime. It was in November 1935 that Shapiro became aware of a story circulating through the organized crime grapevine that Dutch Schultz—gunned down in Newark just a few weeks before— had buried several million dollars in the Catskill Mountains and that one of his men had sketched a map to the exact spot.

Shapiro figured he knew the Catskills as well as anyone—after all, he had spent considerable time over the years at the Plaza, as well as the Rock Hill and Loch Sheldrake Country Clubs—and he thought he could find the treasure with little trouble. All he needed was the map. He discovered that one of Schultz's henchmen, Lulu Rosenkrantz, had given the map to a friend of his, a penny-ante gangster named Marty Krompier, with instructions to keep it in a safe place. Shapiro was told that Krompier carried the map in his wallet everywhere he went.

Shapiro ordered his men to kill Krompier and to bring the map back to him. Some of Shapiro's men followed Krompier into a Manhattan barbershop one afternoon, shot him, and took the map. Forthwith, it was delivered to the anxious Shapiro. But Gurrah was in for a surprise: The map showed the location of the treasure, all right, but the area it described wasn't in Sullivan County. Schultz had owned a home near Phoenicia, and the map clearly indicated that the money had been hidden near there—in the *Ulster County* Catskills.

"These ain't the Catskills," an enraged Shapiro reportedly said, not immediately grasping the geography lesson he had just received. Convinced that the whole thing was just a prank, he tore the map into little pieces and flung them into the air, never to be seen again.

Shapiro continued to travel regularly to Sullivan County—the only Catskills he knew—unaware of just how close he might have been to the millions Dutch Schultz reportedly had stashed.

CRIME AND PUNISHMENT

Other maps have surfaced from time to time, though no one has ever been able to determine how, and dozens of other gangsters—and treasure hunters in general—have flocked to Phoenicia over the years in search of Dutch Schultz's buried treasure.

Mob Legend Waxey Pops Up at Rocky's

THE REGULARS at Rocky's Italian Garden were really giving me a hard time. Apparently my columns about Waxey Gordon's arrest in White Lake had been a hot topic at the Monticello restaurant, and I had the misfortune of arriving there for dinner while it was still fresh in their minds.

Rocky started off by greeting me with, "I saw a guy in White Lake this morning who looked a lot like Waxey Gordon. Do you suppose it's possible?"

Larry, the bartender, couldn't resist joining in. "You like to write about that kind of stuff, don't you?" he asked. "All those columns on Murder, Incorporated, and now Waxey Gordon. Who'll be next? Lepke?"

A big guy at the bar would not be outdone. "That was an interesting column about Waxey Gordon getting arrested in White Lake," he said, "but you never really explained much about Gordon, himself. What was he like? Why was he here? Was he just visiting? Did he have ties to the area, or what?"

"Who's this Waxey Gordon, anyway?" one of the young waitresses asked. "Is he a ballplayer or something?"

Outnumbered, I delivered a brief biography of Waxey Gordon.

Gordon was one of crimedom's big-leaguers in the 1920s and early '30s. He was born Irving Wexler, and made his early reputation as a pickpocket on the Lower East Side; he purportedly earned his nickname because of his dexterity—he could slide the wallets out of people's pockets as if they were coated with wax.

Gordon became a criminal superstar during Prohibition, eventually running a distillery in this area which, along with similar establishments in New Jersey and Philadelphia, supplied illegal booze to a network of bootleggers around the country. It is said that these and other illicit activities provided him with an annual income of between one and two million dollars, as well as a posh suite of offices on Manhattan's 42nd Street.

He engaged in a well-known shooting war with another rum-runner, Meyer Lansky, in a feud which became known in the underworld as The War of the Jews, and he later carried on a bitter and bloody feud with fellow bootlegger Dutch Schultz. This war with Schultz led, somewhat indirectly, to the murder of Gordon henchman Chink Sherman.

Both Schultz and Lansky (who was then aligned with Bugsy Siegel in the deadly enforcement group known as the Bug and Meyer Gang) possessed more firepower than Gordon, however, and Waxey's prominence began to wane. He was indicted on income tax evasion charges in 1932, no doubt set up by someone in Meyer Lansky's employ, and was on the lam in White Lake when picked up on those charges. Gordon was convicted in December 1933 and sentenced to ten years in Leavenworth. When he left prison in 1940, his fortune was largely gone, and he pledged to go straight.

"Waxey Gordon is dead," he reportedly said. "From now on, it's Irving Wexler, salesman."

Unfortunately for Gordon, that wasn't to be. What Irving Wexler, salesman, was selling, apparently, was drugs—and penny-ante stuff at that. He was arrested again in 1951 and sentenced to twenty-five years to life for small-time trafficking in narcotics. He died in Alcatraz prison in June 1952, about as far from being a crime czar as anyone could get.

For many people who lived in this area in the 1920s and early '30s, however—and for the regulars at Rocky's Italian Garden, too—Waxey Gordon will always be remembered as the big-shot criminal who was arrested in White Lake in 1932.

OTHER SULLIVAN COUNTY BOOKS
PUBLISHED BY PURPLE MOUNTAIN PRESS

Remember the Catskills
Tales by a Recovering Hotelkeeper
Esterita "Cissie" Blumberg

Popular columnist Cissie Blumberg shares her unfailingly warm and often humorous stories of a lifetime spent catering to city guests in the Catskill Mountains.

Dear Cissie —

I remember the Catskills — I remember Green Acres — I remember your kindness — But most of all, I remember your blintzes — Almost as good as my mother's — Reading the book I could taste the sour cream.

I thank God for placing these mountains so close to New York City — Route 17 was my highway to show business — It was my training ground — It gave me my career. I send you a hug for keeping the Catskills alive with this fine book.   —*Red Buttons*

Dear Cissie —

What I recall most about the Catskills is a small hotel called Avon Lodge in a unique little village called Woodridge. Certainly those of us who "played" the mountain resorts had a wonderful opportunity to refine our craft before audiences who were more than willing to be entertained. That experience was part of growing in the business and in life. I am pleased to know that the stories of the hotels and the Catskill towns will live on in this book.   —*Sid Caesar*

OTHER SULLIVAN COUNTY BOOKS
PUBLISHED BY PURPLE MOUNTAIN PRESS

Stephen Crane:
SULLIVAN COUNTY TALES AND SKETCHES

Edited and with an Introduction by
R. W. Stallman
Preface by John Conway

This collection will hold a special attraction for those interested in Sullivan County as the wellspring for Stephen Crane's development as a writer. Here, in his earliest published pieces, there is clear evidence of Crane's painterly and impressionistic style and his addiction to color adjectives, metaphor, and symbol. Also seen are the seeds of themes which were soon to appear in *Maggie: A Girl of the Streets* and *The Red Badge of Courage*, the former noted for its grotesqueries and the latter for its psychological probing of character.

R. W. Stallman is the author of *Stephen Crane: A Biography* and has edited several volumes of Crane's works.

Also:
THE RED BADGE OF COURAGE
Introduced and Historically Annotated by Charles La Rocca

The editor presents compelling evidence that the action in Crane's famous novel was based on the Civil War experiences of the 124th New York State Volunteers, Orange County's regiment, whose veterans Crane was known to have interviewed. "Though many editions have historical introductions, these page-by-page commentaries make this a superior choice." —*Library Journal*

These and other Purple Mountain Press regional classics are available at bookstores or from the publisher.